INTERPERSONAL COMMUNICATION

A Cross-Disciplinary Approach

INTERPERSONAL COMMUNICATION
A Cross-Disciplinary Approach

By

Arthur Solomon, Ph.D.

Director, Communication Program
Antioch College
Yellow Springs, Ohio

with

Steven Perry

and

Robert Devine

Staff Members, Communication Program
Antioch College
Yellow Springs, Ohio

CHARLES C THOMAS • PUBLISHER
Springfield • Illinois • U.S.A.

Published and Distributed throughout the World by

CHARLES C THOMAS • PUBLISHER

BANNERSTONE HOUSE

301-327 East Lawrence Avenue, Springfield, Illinois, U.S.A.

NATCHEZ PLANTATION HOUSE

735 North Atlantic Boulevard, Fort Lauderdale, Florida, U.S.A.

With THOMAS BOOKS *careful attention is given to all details of
manufacturing and design. It is the Publisher's desire to present books
that are satisfactory as to their physical qualities and artistic possibilities
and appropriate for their particular use.* THOMAS BOOKS *will be true
to those laws of quality that assure a good name and good will.*

INTRODUCTION

An Undergraduate Workshop in Interpersonal Communication

THIS MANUAL, based on the Communication Program at Antioch College, has a dual purpose. It is a progress report of our experience to date in teaching the workshop, and it contains enough illustrative ideas for reference use in other settings and other programs of this kind.

In February of 1965, Antioch College, through its Office of Program Development and Research in Education, proposed to the Jack Wolfram Foundation that the college institute a program of courses, seminars, or workshops designed to help students develop more effective communication ability. The program would emphasize the psychological determinants of communication as well as the more traditional speech and speaking skills.

It was designed to provide students with a variety of learning experiences in interpersonal relations, in group process skills, and in oral communication. Small groups, designed to assure a climate in which students could experiment with new ways of behaving and relating, were to constitute the primary learning context. New media for teaching-learning would also be explored and evaluated.

An initial grant was awarded by the Jack Wolfram Foundation and supplemented by the college to provide staff and facilities for development. During the summer of 1965, a project-planning group elaborated patterns of course organization, ideas for instructional materials, outlines of plans for evaluation and research, and an approach for the use of videotape recording.

Remote control videotape recording equipment was to be installed to aid students in each of the proposed learning areas, to aid in staff training, and to serve in research and evaluation.

Two pilot offerings of the program were initiated as a workshop in Antioch's experimental first-year program in the fall of 1965. The first year of operation centered on the development of methodology for teaching and the design and application of materials for study, which included a bibliography of literature, tapes, and films. In the pages that follow, we wish to share some of these experiences and findings.

Acknowledgments for assistance, support, and encouragement must start with Mr. Jack Wolfram, whose Foundation made the program possible and whose personal assistance in our planning—through frequent participation and observation of our efforts—is even more appreciated. The program is highly indebted to Dr. Samuel Baskin, Director of Antioch's Office of Program Development and Research in Education; to the original members of the planning group: Mrs. Fressa Inman, Dr. William Mullins, Mr. Leon Segal, Miss Beverly Price, Mr. Robert Green, Mrs. Nancy Teepen; and to our many student assistants for their help in planning the program and preparing this manual. Special acknowledgment must be made to Mr. Alfred M. Sinder of Dayton Communications for his assistance in designing, installing, and nurturing our videotape facility above and beyond contractual agreements and indeed into the area of interpersonal communications.

ARTHUR SOLOMON

CONTENTS

Part I

INTERPERSONAL COMMUNICATION

A Cross-Disciplinary Approach

DESCRIPTION OF THE PROGRAM

Beginnings

T HE CURRENT ANTIOCH COMMUNICATION PROGRAM is the outgrowth of many years of experimentation with basic "encounter
groups," small-group-functioning classes, and more conventional
courses. Extracurricular "T-groups" (training groups), on the
National Training Laboratory's model, have been sporadically offered to both faculty and students for a number of years. This
small-group approach was introduced by Douglas McGregor when
he came from Massachusetts Institute of Technology to assume the
Antioch presidency in 1951. An academic methodology was formalized almost twenty years ago when a course in small-group
functioning was sponsored by the Psychology Department and the
Dean of Student's Office. Focusing on the group, these classes
stressed the social psychology of small-group interaction and collaborative processes of leadership, decision-making, and problem-
solving.

Courses in basic voice and diction, theater speech, and public
speaking were also part of the curriculum but were traditionally
limited to a skill and technique approach.

It was from these roots that the communication program sought
to formalize a variety of experiences in a new course that would
recognize the interdisciplinary nature of the communication process
and bring relevant components together.

The project-planning group of students, faculty, and staff attempted to design a more comprehensive program and to renew
the search for those components which would make communication both meaningful and effective to the rather select upper-
middle-class student attracted to an experimental college like
Antioch.

The Wolfram Foundation sponsors agreed with our planning
group that communication meant more than persuasion or skill in

speech, and that a new course should incorporate recent findings from the sociology and psychology of interactive communication.

The planning group examined a wide range of relevant subject matter, which included group dynamics, semantics, linguistics, group counseling, sensitivity training, mass media, and communication theory and research. From this investigation some fundamental questions emerged:

> What factors are basic to learning new communicative behavior? How can students learn to become listeners and speakers? How is a climate conducive to communication created? What are the personal and social barriers in communicating, and how can they be surmounted? How can ease, fluency, and confidence in self-expression be achieved? How are honest disagreement and conflict to be dealt with so that problems may be solved, and decisions made with some degree of mutual understanding and acceptance?

→ Agreeing that communication rests ultimately upon total interactive behavior, the planning group examined its basic assumptions about the connection between interpersonal relations and communication. These assumptions were gathered from many sources and served as guidelines for further planning of course structure and course components. These are the assumptions which guided this search:

> Receptivity and response appear to increase when the effort to understand oneself and others is encouraged. To communicate interactively is to become aware of one's own perceptions and distortions and to see another's responses, values, and attitudes. An individual's needs and attitudes, in turn, determine his perception, his interaction, and ultimately his communicative behavior.
>
> An individual learns new communicative behavior as his awareness expands, as he is able to relate theory and practice to his own needs, and as he fully participates in significant interactive experiences.
>
> In the absence of threat, a clearer perception of self and of others becomes possible, especially if speaker and listener respond with openness and trust, and then spontaneous participation and learning are more apt to occur on both the emotional and intellectual levels.
>
> Feelings generated about the verbal and nonverbal behavior of others and of self can provide useful, objective data for study.
>
> Small groups, in an atmosphere of trust and without the coercion of authoritarian structure, can more easily provide the interactive experience and encouragement for new communicative attempts.

Out of these questions and basic assumptions, the following course components were determined.

Speaking skills were to be included, but only as one component within an overall communication program which emphasized both the interpersonal and dynamic aspects of communication as well as the medium of verbal exchange.

Small-group process skills were deemed essential because so much of current social interaction occurs within the small-group setting of conference, discussion, and committee meetings, while so little sensitivity and skill are generally brought to bear in these encounters.

Interpersonal communication would provide the participants the experience of becoming more aware of themselves and of one another as people with feelings and sensibilities.

It was the expectation of the planning group that the skills, perceptions, and understandings necessary for meaningful and effective communication could be experienced and learned. It was toward confirmation of this hypothesis that the Antioch Communication Program was undertaken.

Speech and Speaking Skills

Introduction

A basic component of our program in communication provided opportunities for skill-training and practice in speech and speaking. It seemed a reasonable hypothesis that if ideas and feelings were to be effectively exchanged, minimal standards of intelligibility, expression, and organization should be required. To this end, specific units were designed for voice and diction improvement, oral reading expression, and formal speaking to improve organization and delivery. This wide range was attempted on the assumption that students participating in this program would have no additional training opportunities in speaking skills at Antioch.

The speaking skills design incorporated a diagnostic and background unit prerequisite to the practice and performance sections that were to follow.

Diagnostic and Background Unit

At the initial meeting, audiotape and videotape recordings were made of each individual's reading and speaking. The recorded material consisted of a "cold-running-speech" sample, followed by the reading of "emotional poetic material," and concluded with a short impromptu speech. The material used is included in the course syllabus (Appendix A).

During each recording, an analysis of voice, diction, fluency,

expressiveness, and poise of the student was made. Later playbacks
of the audio and video recordings allowed each student to see and
hear his speaking manner and communicative behavior. The video
recording allowed observation of nonverbal components such as
posture, movement, gesture, facial expression, and overall carriage.
In addition, the tapes provided comparative data for later progress
checks. After this diagnostic work, lectures, readings, films, and
tapes were assigned or presented to provide some understanding
of the physiological mechanism and the communicative, phonetic,
and aesthetic aspects of the speaking function.

Voice and Diction Skills

This unit consisted of group practice with voice and diction exercises and individual oral presentations before the class, followed
by critiques. Daily practice periods were assigned, along with listening exercises and reports.

The complete syllabus (Appendix A) divided the program into
three weeks of speaking skills, three weeks of group process skills,
and four weeks of interpersonal communication. In addition to objectives, procedures, and calendar, the syllabus contains recording
material, a voice-training analysis form, three pages of speech exercises for daily practice, a public-speaking outline organization
which condenses main points in speech preparation, and finally a
brief annotated bibliography covering the three areas of the course.

Using the "sung-vowel approach", the vocal factors of resonance,
projection, and tone duration are developed through singing techniques. By reciting the words after they are sung, singing qualities
can be retained and utilized in the spoken voice. This approach
results in an open and relaxed jaw and throat, a slow rate of speech,
a wide range of pitch, and a well-projected tone. Clearness of articulation is achieved through emphasis on individual sounds and on
the physical movements producing them. Ear-training and listening
discrimination are achieved by having students pay close attention
to tonal qualities and differences between speakers—a function of
the critiques, listening assignments, and class audiotapes. Individual
conferences are also available to aid students with specific problems.

Oral Reading Skills

The ability to read aloud with ease, fluency, and clarity is a skill that can be improved measurably with practice. The basic elements of oral interpretation were conveyed through lectures, discussions, demonstrations, and the critiques of class presentations. Daily assignments and class performance provided the necessary practice.

Oral reading skills follow naturally from voice and diction improvement exercises. The former stresses the expression of ideas and feelings from the printed page, whereas voice and diction stress the basic raw material of vocal production.

Because the major emphasis here was given to oral expression, the aesthetic and intellectual appreciation of the literature was given only cursory attention. Lecture demonstrations stressed the importance of phrasing, emphasis, subordination, and effective expression through vocal variety and emotional meanings. The auditing of poetry, drama, and other professional recordings was assigned. Presentations of prose and poetry, followed by critiques and recorded playbacks, gave the student practice opportunities before an audience.

Specific aids to the beginning oral reader included assignments in interpretation texts, analysis and critique forms, tape recordings, oral presentations, and individual conferences where required.

Formal Speaking

A unit on the skills of organizing and delivering formal speaking presentations was included in the program. Three minimal steps were felt necessary: the preparation of researched material into an appropriate organizational pattern; a written outline form, developing the material in sequential and orderly steps; and the delivery of the talk before an audience.

To aid in organizing and outlining, a two-page form was put together from summarized material found in standard speech texts. The outline gave the student some basic, albeit simplified, information in speech preparation. In addition, chapters on organization and outlining were assigned for supplementary reading. (See Appendix A.) A brief introductory lecture explained the different types of speeches and the value and methods of organizing and outlining.

At least three speeches were assigned, beginning with a demonstration speech in which a physical object or other material was used for illustrative purposes. This introduced formal speechmaking with minimal stress since the attention of the audience was divided between the speaker and his visual material; it provided the beginning student with something physical to do, usually by a sequence of proscribed movements; and it contained its own built-in, organizational pattern. The second speech was informative, and the final speech persuasive or argumentative. For all three speeches, students were asked to outline their material, write a central statement, and indicate their purpose in giving the speech.

Videotapes were made of initial and final speeches, and of others when time allowed. This not only provided the speaker with immediate feedback of his voice and delivery, but it also permitted an objective appraisal of his nonverbal communication. This use of videotape recording was immediately helpful to the students and later much appreciated by the instructor, because it afforded an objective measure of progress when initial and final recordings were compared.

Evaluation of the Speaking-skill Component

The inclusion of the speaking-skill component naturally leads to a high degree of condensation and intensity, which has advantages as well as disadvantages. It puts the speaking skills into a larger context of immediate relevancy and application. It also provides at least a minimal exposure to basic theory, practice, and performance techniques that can be further developed according to individual needs. Such condensation also eliminates much elaboration and repetition that bright, highly motivated students find redundant.

However reasonable in theory, the inclusion of the speech-skill component within the large communication context is difficult in practice due to limitations of time and student interest. It was found that students interested in interpersonal communication had little or no patience with skill-training exercises or formal presentations. The relevance, the immediacy, and the impact of the interpersonal component overshadowed the technique and skill approach. Students felt that the necessarily didactic teaching method employed in speech training compared unfavorably with the "group-centered approach" of the other sections. In addition, it could be argued that the auditory and visual evidence of improvement in poise, self-confidence, and expression at the end of the course could be attributed as much to the other experiences of the course as to the skill-training component.

During one quarter, a few students voluntarily chose to participate in the skill section, which continued separately for the entire quarter. The speech results were far better than when all students had been required to spend the first three weeks in speaking practice and exercises.

The comparison of audio recordings made at the beginning and at end of the workshop each quarter gave a clear indication of speech improvement for those who practiced conscientiously. The inclusion of a speaking-skill section was not unsuccessful, as the student evaluations will attest and as indicated by audiotape recordings. Nevertheless, the cost in instructor time, and the slight to theory and practice material, comprise an injustice to both student and subject matter. It would appear wise and in the best interest of the student, the speech-skill subject matter, and the rest of the communication program, to offer speech and speaking skills as a separate course, perhaps as a component of the total program but not in the same workshop.

Student Evaluations

The following excerpts of student reactions were selected from the final evaluation reports which each student was requested to write at termination of the workshop. The students were asked to evaluate the subjective effect of the various course components. These comments refer to speaking or listening:

"From this course, I have come to realize my own need to improve my voice, and this is something for a stubborn person like me."

"I have always found it difficult to speak in groups; but this time it was much easier. I even spoke my thoughts at several meetings outside of class. I feel this represents a good beginning."

"I do not believe I improved my voice significantly, but I did overcome a good deal of my nervousness, allowing me to experiment with more expressive delivery patterns."

"I said in the beginning of the workshop that I wanted to learn how to talk, but the lesson I got was more valuable than that: I learned that as long as I believed I could talk effectively, that belief made it so. It gave me the ability to really say what I meant."

"I no longer choke and gasp for breath when speaking or reading."

"My goals in this seminar have certainly been met. I had hoped to gain more confidence in myself in order to express myself better. I had also hoped that I would learn to enunciate more clearly and develop a more pleasing voice quality. In my opinion, my hopes have become realities."

"Although I am not a verbal person, I now find that when I wish to speak, I can do so freely and comfortably . . . your conference with me when we discussed my 'clenched teeth' manner of speaking has been very helpful. As I improve my speaking voice, I will gain greater confidence in my ability to speak."

"I feel that, besides those speech skills I have already mentioned, I am modulating my voice more, and this makes me much more self-assured. I don't feel that I squawk or scream as much as I used to."

"I learned that there are more forms of communication than the spoken word, and that by noticing the actions and expressions of the person talking, it is possible to learn more about what he is thinking than by listening only to what he is saying."

"I must admit that I really did not get much of it (speech lessons) aside from a realization that speech has greater creative potentialities and can be more dynamic than I had expected."

"For me the most important of these changes is the relative ease with which I can now speak in groups. I no longer feel completely inhibited in expressing my reactions and ideas. I speak with greater self-confidence and less self-consciousness."

Group Process Skills

Introduction

For students to learn group process skills, the functioning of the group itself became the object of study and analysis. The intent was to provide a setting where practice could lead to greater understanding and increased competence by aiding the student in developing certain participatory and observational skills.

The specific objectives were to assist the students in their understanding of small-group functioning and the processes by which groups make decisions and accomplish objectives. In the end, we hoped that the student would increase the accuracy of his perceptions of group difficulties, would increase his understanding and practice of leadership functions, would enhance his problem-solving and decision-making skills, and would communicate more confidently and competently as a participant in various group settings.

These objectives called for new roles for students and instructor within a small, group-centered learning environment, where responsibility for progress and change could be shared by all participants.

The Small Group as a Context for Learning

We assumed that students entered this program because they wanted to learn—that they were willing to risk discomfort by examining their basic assumptions and that they were willing to participate without the customary dependence upon an instructor. Generally, our experience supported these assumptions about the students and defined the parameters of the instructor's responsibilities.

People cannot fully learn from one another until they have established a measure of rapport—some degree of mutual trust, support, and respect. When the students trust others to respect their own personal rate of growth and learning, when they realize they have support if they experience difficulties in new explorations, then the climate is conducive to learning. Here, each member could confront several new views of himself and have an opportunity to develop new insights and behaviors.

The instructor has an important task in this respect. Because he is active, initially, in structuring the activities and explaining the concepts, his behavior will in large measure influence the climate of the group. The instructor's role is to teach, but to teach in a special way. It is not sufficient for him to expound cognitive material; he must be able to present the concepts and constructs in an approach that guides and evokes rather than lectures and instructs. His behavior can become a model for identification and emulation by group members. The small group itself can thus become the main resource and the context for the learning experience.

Unit Structure

The syllabus, first class meeting, group size, and instructors all produce an initial impact on the students. When the time available was limited, it was found preferable for instructors to assume initially a greater share of the planning for beginning meetings and activities.

The sample syllabus below reflects the general approach we have taken: the processes of the course receive as much attention as the information content. The students are included in the planning of specific meeting units. The objectives are specific without unduly restricting the road the particular group or individual can take. The resources are made explicit; the students know what is available, and the instructors are permitted to become co-managers instead of sources of structure.

Sample Syllabus
WORKSHOP IN GROUP PROCESS

I. Objectives
  A. To understand the theory and practice of small-group functioning
  B. To develop specific skills and competence
    1. Accurately perceiving and diagnosing group difficulties
    2. Observation of member roles
    3. Understanding and practicing leadership functions
    4. Problem-solving and decision-making
  C. To manage the current task of developing a learning group

II. Procedures
  A. Shared decision-making about group goals, use of resources and procedures
  B. Resources available for scheduling
    1. Weekly two-hour meeting in studio
    2. Videotaping and playback times
    3. Readings from bibliography/reports of readings
    4. Films and audiotapes
    5. Team meetings for projects
    6. Group-skill exercises
    7. Questionnaires
  C. Evaluation process and conferences; objective and subjective measures for evaluating change in skills, understanding, and behavior

III. Calendar of meeting plans and assignments
  A. Planning and organizational meeting; proposed topics
    1. Leadership
    2. Decision-making
    3. Collaborative behavior
    4. Group observation assignment
    5. Team projects
    6. Other

IV. Bibliography (list of books, journals, tapes, and films available to students as supplements)

As instructors, we found that by preparing the syllabus, a few role-play exercises, brief lectures or "lecturettes", and reaction forms before the course started, we were able to devote more time to individual students and to the development of each particular group. Our intent was to prepare for a variety of approaches within a general structure but still to remain free from commitment to a particular sequence of activities.

Lecturettes

Lecturettes are short presentations given by the instructor at an appropriate and useful moment. Over the time the workshop has been offered, we have found that some topics are almost always relevant to a group's development; these provided us with a useful repertoire of materials. We read over the prepared lecturette notes, duplicated the material, and kept copies on hand. We were then ready to introduce the material and information—when and if appropriate.

To give an idea of the topics prepared for, we are including a list of titles and descriptions of some material we used.[1]

How Are Decisions Made in Groups? A diagram classifying group decisions (from "Plop to Consensus") based on the work of Bass, with a short discussion of the behaviors that lead to decision-making and the criteria used for judging the effectiveness of a decision.

Johari Window. A model of social-emotional relationships based on increasing self-awareness. Outlines the dynamics of interaction, discusses socialization and self-control, and sets out conditions for psychological growth.

Goals and Meta-goals. A partial list of the conventional goals of higher education contrasted with similar but more dynamic goals of interpersonal education. Includes decision-making, commitment, problem-solving, criteria of successful learning, and sources of information.

Dilemmas of Leadership. Problems arising from discrepancies between what we say is "right" and what we do in practice. Includes a summary of hierarchy of needs, McGregor's X and Y theories of human behavior, and Schmidt and Tannenbaum's autocrat-abdicrat

---

[1]*NTL Skill Exercise Workshop,* Washington, D.C., National Education Association, 1958. Ideas, notes, and examples of this material are available from:

The NTL Institute for Applied Behavioral Science
1201 Sixteenth Street, N.W.
Washington, D.C. 20036
and
The Human Relations Institute
University of Cincinnati
Cincinnati, Ohio 45221

leadership continuum.

Group Processes. Notes group task functions—the four functions which are objective or goal-oriented, process or structure-oriented, personnel or group maintenance functions, and summarizing oriented functions.

Integrative and Distributive Social Situations. Discusses cooperative and competitive strategies, the assumptions each strategy makes and some of their effects, and raises questions of appropriateness and choice.

Communication. A complex overview. Discusses a multi-level approach to a group task level/maintenance level, work level, emotional level, surface level/hidden level, etc. Discusses behavior as result of multiple motivations. Introduces concepts of input-output and interaction analysis.

Because instructional information of this kind tended to create a debate-define-discuss-clarify cycle that was a step removed from the group's immediate experiences and behaviors, we used this cognitive material input when least obtrusive.

All of our assumptions about increasing skills in effective group participation are built on the student's role as an observing participant: the opportunities for growth and learning derived from the student's abilities to recognize and understand what was going on within the group and within himself. It was equally important for the instructor to see himself as another participating observer. It was in this way that the students experienced a learning relationship with an adult who was responsive to them and their needs and growth, and, most important, who had shown a willingness to earn his group membership on the same terms.

The First Meeting

Typically, only the instructor was involved in planning and structuring the first meeting. The particular combination of objectives, rationale, and activities had to be fitted to the unique characteristics of the setting, the group membership, and the instructor.

While the specific objectives varied, the first meeting usually focused on members' interests and needs, the groups' purposes and requirements, reasons for the small-group format, and the special requirements of membership in a student-centered course.

Planning for this first meeting included some consideration of these questions:

> How much experience do the members have in the area of group dynamics?
> What is a reasonable expectation for member participation?
> What pace is necessary to meet the academic goals in the total time available?
> Is the involvement to be focused on the conceptual or emotional level, or both?
> Will evaluation be based on information acquisition or on increased behavior responses?
> What is the group size and composition?
> What time blocks are established within the total course time?
> In what activities would members be best prepared to engage?
> How flexible should the plan be?

Following the first meeting, these same points should be reconsidered in light of what has happened, and with some attention to the first post-meeting reaction forms.

FIRST MEETING PLAN (SAMPLE)

Micro-Exercise Discussion and Planning

Objectives: To start the group by an initial, involving experience, to get acquainted, to begin planning for later meetings.

Format: Micro-exercise group divided in half by odd and even numbers.
  a. "Evens" meet in inner circle for 10-15 minutes to discuss expectations of course, expectations of self, individual concerns, immediate reactions to course and other members, with "Odds" in outer circle, observing a partner.
  b. Reverse positions, discussing same topics for 15 minutes.
  c. Pairs meet for 15 minutes to share experience.
  d. Group discusses the micro-exercise for 10-20 minutes.
  e. Group plans where to begin at the next meeting, 5-15 minutes.
  f. Distribute, complete, and collect post-meeting reaction forms if used (5-10 minutes).

Notes: This plan assumes 50 or 80 minutes of meeting time, ten or twelve student members and staff, involvement by all members, and dual focus on the emotional feeling level and the intellectual concept level.

This plan establishes instructors as co-participants and as leadership resources, expectations of high participation by all members, and that goals and processes will be established by the individuals and by the group.

Role-play Exercises

We used role-playing techniques as a primary tool for providing group-skills experience. Role plays which emphasized leadership, decision-making, problem-solving, and conflict-handling were developed or modified for group use.

Our role-playing involved establishing a situation and having group members act out their interpretations of particular roles: you are the elected chairman of this committee; or you must try to accomplish a predetermined goal wherein you have an important conference in twenty minutes and will push for a rapid solution. The structure was simple or elaborate, the individual's roles well-defined or very open-ended, or whatever worked best with various groups.

We found that exercises provided an opportunity for behavior experimentation when they were clearly established as safe games. For similar reasons, we experienced considerable resistance on the part of some students to "wasting time on make-believe activities." Occasionally, by revising the situations to fit current campus events, we could add an element of reality without losing the security of the game. All of the exercises provided a shared experience based on actual events. This added common data on behavior which were useful in later meetings, in addition to the value of the skills acquired.

Much of the role-play material focused on decision-making, shared-leadership skills, group-maintenance and goal-oriented behavior. When students gained an understanding of these areas and some proficiency in these activities, they could then effectively develop their own exercises.

We are including a description of the "Moon Crash" role play to illustrate a goal-oriented exercise and also a typical methodology we found useful. Some of books and articles listed in the general bibliography provide more information on the role-play technique and additional examples. In most cases, we found it most valuable to work up our own exercises to fit our groups.

The Moon Crash Exercise is a fairly simple role play in its basic form. Without embellishment, it can be used as a diagnostic exercise as a means of establishing the problem areas the group will need to focus on in the future, and as a test of leadership, problem-solving behavior, and decision-making.

MOON CRASH EXERCISE

Instructions: You are a member of a space crew originally scheduled to rendezvous with a mother ship on the lighted surface of the moon. Due to mechanical difficulties, however, your ship was forced to land at a spot some 200 miles from the rendezvous point. During re-entry and landing, much of the equipment aboard was damaged and, since survival depends upon reaching the mother ship, the most critical items available must be chosen for the 200-mile trip. Below are listed the 15 items left intact and undamaged after landing. Your task is to rank order them in terms of their importance for your crew in allowing them to reach the rendezvous point. Place the number 1 by the most important, and so on through number 15, the least important.

Box of matches	Stellar map
Food concentrate	Life raft
50 feet of nylon rope	Magnetic compass
Parachute silk	5 gallons of water
Portable heating unit	Signal flares
Two .45 calibre pistols	First-aid kit containing
One case dehydrated milk	injection needles
Two 100-lb. tanks of oxygen	Solar-powered FM receiver-transmitter

After appropriate comments to introduce the exercise, the instruction sheets were handed out. The instructor explained that he had no additional information, that he would be observing the exercise, that the time the group had to complete the task would be thirty minutes, and that the group should attempt to arrive at a consensus by resolving any honest diversity of viewpoints. Following the role-play experience, the instructor had three options.

First, the instructor could share his observations of how the group members went about completing the task. This moved the group into an immediate process discussion. Questions of leadership, responsibility, participation, efficiency, group climate, and so on, could be illustrated in the ensuing discussion.

Second, the instructor could distribute the Group Evaluation Form and/or the Individual Evaluation Form. After the forms had been filled out, the questions and responses themselves would serve as a basis for discussion and analysis. This approach again moved the group into a process discussion, but in a more structured way.

GROUP EVALUATION FORM
Name:
(1 on the scale is very low; 5 is very high)

1. How far did the group get in making a decision?	1 2 3 4 5
2. To what extent was the group stymied for lack of information?	1 2 3 4 5
3. Was the objective clearly stated or understood?	1 2 3 4 5
4. Was the decision-making process efficient and systematic?	1 2 3 4 5
5. Were alternative decisions considered?	1 2 3 4 5
6. Were minority views acknowledged?	1 2 3 4 5
7. Was interest maintained?	1 2 3 4 5
8. Were member contributions and information directed to the problem?	1 2 3 4 5
9. Did a leader emerge?	1 2 3 4 5
10. Were you satisfied with group performance in respect to the following:	
a. Quality of the decision?	1 2 3 4 5
b. Group process and procedure?	1 2 3 4 5

INDIVIDUAL EVALUATION FORM

Name:

A. Were you satisfied with the way leadership was handled in this decision? I felt:
9. Completely satisfied.
8. Quite satisfied.
7. Moderately satisfied.
6. A little more satisifed than dissatisfied.
5. Neither very satisfied nor very dissatisfied.
4. A little more dissatisfied than satisfied.
3. Moderately dissatisfied.
2. Quite dissatisfied.
1. Completely dissatisfied.

B. How satisfied did you feel with the amount and quality of your participation in reaching a decision? I felt:
9. Completely satisfied.
8. Quite satisfied.
7. Moderately satisfied.
6. A little more satisfied than dissatisfied.
5. Neither very satisfied nor very dissatisfied.
4. A little more dissatisfied than satisfied.
3. Moderately dissatisfied.
2. Quite dissatisfied.
1. Completely dissatisfied.

C. How much responsibility for the work did you feel? I felt:
9. Completely responsible.
8. Quite responsible.
7. Moderately responsible.
6. A little more responsible than not responsible.
5. Neither very responsible nor very irresponsible.
4. A little more irresponsible than responsible.
3. Moderately irresponsible.
2. Quite irresponsible.
1. Completely irresponsible.

D. How committed do you feel to the decision you made as a group? I felt:
9. Completely committed.
8. Quite committed.
7. Moderately committed.
6. A little more committed than uncommitted.
5. Neither very committed nor very uncommitted.
4. A little more uncommitted than committed.
3. Moderately uncommitted.
2. Quite uncommitted.
1. Completely uncommitted.

E. How much frustration did you feel during the work on the decision? I felt:
9. Completely frustrated.
8. Quite frustrated.
7. Moderately frustrated.
6. A little more frustrated than approving.
5. Neither very frustrated nor very approving.
4. A little more approving than frustrated.
3. Moderately approving.
2. Quite approving.
1. Completely approving.

F. How good was the decision you made as a group? It was:
9. The best possible.
8. Quite good.
7. Moderately good.
6. A little more good than bad.
5. Neither very good nor very bad.
4. A little more bad than good.
3. Moderately bad.
2. Quite bad.
1. The worst possible.

Third, the same form, or forms, could be used and immediately tabulated and displayed to the group. This structured a very definite focus on the group's assessment of its performance and the total impact of the activity.

Whatever the option taken, the instructor was in a position to help the group to reformulate the discussion into planning activities for subsequent meetings. This approach had greater meaning to the group when it was accurate, clear, and drawn from the experience, rather than trying to fit what had happened in the exercise into a predetermined plan which would negate the group experience.

Group Self-appraisal

The basic form, often called the Post-Meeting Reaction form, or PMR, focuses on the individual's assessment of the meeting and his own participation. The forms were distributed, completed, and returned at the end of each group meeting. We found, through the use of forms, a methodical way of securing data on the members' reactions to the meeting, the group, or the other members of the group. The two scales and five questions given below represent the latest revision we are presently using.

POST MEETING REACTION FORM

Date: Name:

1. How did you feel about this meeting in general? (Circle one number)

1	2	3	4	5	6	7
Very Dissatisfied	Somewhat dissatisfied	Dissatisfied	Neutral	Satisfied	Quite satisfied	Very satisfied

2. Were there times when you wished to speak but did not? (Circle one)

1	2	3	4	5	6	7
Never	Very few times	A few times	Fairly often	Often	Very often	All the time

3. Comments on #1 and #2 above?
4. Which parts of the meeting did you like most? Which least?
5. Which parts *helped* you to participate in the meeting? (Be as specific as possible.)
6. Which parts *hindered* you from taking part in the meeeting? (Be as specific as possible.)
7. What could you do to improve our next meeting?

The second form we used is loosely based on a Group Development Questionnaire used by the National Training Laboratories. This form was used like the PMR or as mid-quarter assessment of attitudes reflecting the group climate and cohesiveness.

Reaction forms were used to move a group that was just starting or was slow in developing, but using it as an assessment technique provided useful information for a well-established group. Summaries of the responses when fed back into the group indicated group or member problems needing attention. At the same time, the summaries defined the range and similarities of member needs, feelings, problems, and perceptions.

GROUP DEVELOPMENT QUESTIONNAIRE

Date: Name:

The following items describe certain attributes of group functioning or group atmosphere. I would like you, in answering each item, to think about how well it describes the group up to this point and *circle* the most appropriate answer.

1. Many members are anxious about the directions the group is taking.

| Strongly disagree | Disagree | Moderately disagree | Undecided | Moderately agree | Agree | Strongly agree |

2. There is a lot of underlying irritation in the group.

| Strongly disagree | Disagree | Moderately disagree | Undecided | Moderately agree | Agree | Strongly agree |

3. The group is avoiding difficult or touchy issues.

| Strongly disagree | Disagree | Moderately disagree | Undecided | Moderately agree | Agree | Strongly agree |

4. The group is very cold and unfriendly.

| Strongly disagree | Disagree | Moderately disagree | Undecided | Moderately agree | Agree | Strongly agree |

5. Many members are withdrawing from whatever the group is doing.

| Strongly disagree | Disagree | Moderately disagree | Undecided | Moderately agree | Agree | Strongly agree |

6. There is a lot of underlying tension in the group.

| Strongly disagree | Disagree | Moderately disagree | Undecided | Moderately agree | Agree | Strongly agree |

7. Many members are angry about what is happening in this group.

| Strongly disagree | Disagree | Moderately disagree | Undecided | Moderately agree | Agree | Strongly agree |

8. Many group members are bored and uninvolved.

| Strongly disagree | Disagree | Moderately disagree | Undecided | Moderately agree | Agree | Strongly agree |

9. The group atmosphere is tense and uncomfortable.

| Strongly disagree | Disagree | Moderately disagree | Undecided | Moderately agree | Agree | Strongly agree |

The reaction forms can be overused and become an escape from the "here and now" authentic, spontaneous, and meaningful interaction and learning. The technique provides additional input for group self-appraisal; it is not a remedy. We found that many groups quickly established an awareness and understanding of themselves which, after a few meetings, made the routine use of reaction forms unnecessary.

Videotape Recording

While the use of television and videotape is covered extensively elsewhere, there is some value in describing its particular use in the group process skills unit. Over many years, work in groups has included the use of audiotape recorders. Currently, the availability of videotape in many similar programs is stimulating new research and new techniques. Our television facility was used for group confrontation, data storage and retrieval, and analysis of group process. The videotapes were made easily accessible to group members for reviewing the general functioning of the group.

We developed three videotape playback formats for use in group process skills development: the general playback, the critical incident playback, and the overview playback. The general playbacks started out with the staff deciding on segments of taped material from meeting A that contained data the group should view at meeting B. The nature of these materials usually either presented problems leading into the topic for meeting B or highlighted areas that might be worked into plans for a later meeting. After the group had been meeting for a while, planning the contents of the playback sessions was usually done by the group.

Later in the program, as the focus of the videotape playbacks became less on content and more on process, the tape-use pattern changed. Focusing on the "why" and "how" of things, rather than on the "what", increased the amount of time spent in discussion and reduced the viewing time. Rather than attempting to review entire meetings, groups started to spend the time in attempting to discern, clarify, and analyze specific points of process. Since the videotape incorporated skills, exercises, and goal-oriented group discussions, the explorations into process tended to produce immediate, significant changes in overt behavior. Questions of under-participation or overparticipation, domination, manipulation, leadership, blocking, and hidden agenda became obvious group issues. Discussing these questions usually had behavioral effects, regardless of whether the issue was resolved.

Immediate playback in the classroom of a critical incident encouraged a second form of group confrontation and feedback while the group was still involved in the interaction. They were thus supplied with feedback data on immediate concerns. The playback could be used for detailed analysis, or the observation alone of the critical incidents was often sufficient to demonstrate the state of the group's growth and development.

Overview playbacks were developed to review, coherently, a series of meetings which dynamically illustrated individual and group changes. The instructors established the themes they wanted shown (leadership, participation, goal-setting, etc.) and the amount of time available for the overview. Tape segments were selected, sequenced, and reviewed. These clips were then run in sequence, with instructor comments for the whole group. Since this was usually scheduled for the middle of the program, this overview became an additional group resource. However, the sequences could be stopped at any point where discussion appeared to be more productive than continued viewing.

It is important to note that this playback format was one of the most significant indirect forms of feedback the staff gave the group. The staff was saying in effect, "These are the most important things we think you have done." When the general tone of the overview demonstrated the problems the group had, the lack of progress and growth, individual difficulties, unsuccessful exercises, or unresolved conflicts, the message was very clear. While there is no "correct" content for a playback, it is easy to excerpt tape segments which give a positive impression unless one maintains awareness of the distortions created by the particular selection of segments.

We have produced a 16-mm film, based somewhat on the format of these overview playbacks, for use in connection with this manual. The material is largely documentary, drawn from actual tapes of the group meetings, and will be available at cost as a demonstration of our program.

Outside Assignments

Each syllabus on group process skills included a selected bibliography of books, films, articles, and audiotapes. Our usual procedure was to review the bibliography and suggest that the participants might find materials noted there which would enrich their classroom activities. We would occasionally request short (1-2 paragraphs) critiques before revising the bibliography. We relied on the student feedback in addition to the usual criteria for book selection to help us revise and upgrade the selection of materials included in our list.

We designed our program to emphasize many things. In choosing our emphases, we deliberately avoided use of extensive assigned reading, or report writing. Thus, our bibliography became only another of the resources available to the participants. We tended to avoid spending meeting time in either discussion of written material or in analysis of behavior in terms of a particular author or a particular psychological framework. Others, in different situations, should seek to find the balance between theory and practice that is fitting and proper in their setting.

Where we did require the completion of assigned academic work, it usually took the form of a three-part assignment to be completed within the middle portion of the course. This consisted of reading selected materials (seldom more than 250-300 pages), an observation and report of two meetings of some regularly scheduled task groups, and a short (5-10 pages) paper on such subjects as the effective group, leadership, and individual membership roles (see Appendix B for assignment details). The student had the option to devise his own assignment on some matter of tangential interest. In all of this assigned work, relevancy and application to the ongoing workshop experience appeared to be a most useful parameter.

Evaluation Techniques

Evaluation in our program took many forms and appeared to a greater or lesser degree in most of the workshop activities. Discussion, videotape playbacks and analysis, logs, reaction forms, psychological tests, self-evaluations, reading reports, papers, and conferences—all had elements of continuous evaluation. Group discussion and analysis, reaction forms, papers, and reading reports have been described. In addition, we used logs, psychological tests, conferences, and self-evaluations.

All student participants were asked to submit a weekly summary or log of their reactions, ideas, and evaluations of the group and their own functioning as a group member. The instructor noted his comments on the logs, which served ultimately as a record of progress, and then returned them to the students. The students were asked to reread and bring their logs to the final evaluation conference. Several times, we found that nonparticipants were saving their responses for their logs. In these cases, we would suggest ways in which these students could make some of their responses in the group during the meeting. In several instances, students were asked not to write logs and concentrate on increasing their verbal participation.

Psychological tests to measure any changes in perception or in interaction with others were administered for experimental evaluation and research. The results of these tests provided additional information and dimensions for the students and instructor to utilize in the final evaluation. These measures are discussed in more detail elsewhere.

In addition to a Self-descriptive Questionnaire for subjective ratings administered at the beginning and end of the workshop, students were asked to evaluate their own progress and any notable behavioral change that they could discern. This evaluation provided much of the material for the final conference. Primarily, we asked the students to review their participation, logs, reaction sheets, and notes, and to assess their perception of their own growth and change in attitude and behavior; to assess their knowledge and understandings of group processes; to assess speaking-skill improvement; and to offer comments on improving the course.

In settings where evaluations are expected to include a grade, some modification of these procedures would be necessary. But it is to be assumed that, under these circumstances, modifications would have been made all along to ensure specific evaluation procedures.

STUDENT EVALUATION EXCERPTS

"I saw the function of the group as an open field for individual experimentation. While I noticed few marked changes in individuals, I think that almost everyone 'tried out' various roles to test how they would be received in a group. This is, of course, a valuable opportunity."

"I found that writing the log helped me to crystallize my feelings about a meeting and that it has been very helpful in looking back. It was also a first step toward stating my concerns to someone—later I was able to verbalize them to the group."

"I no longer think of myself as a 'leader,' but rather as a member of the group—any group. I find myself actually interacting with people in groups."

"We usually tried to understand the reasons for a person's behavior, which reaffirmed his value as a person and not just a machine with ideas to be agreed or disagreed with."

"I can listen less evaluatively and less hostilely to others and feel I can change a group's direction now if I want or need to. I understand much more how people's perceptions affect their communications in, and feelings about, group happenings."

"I have learned a lot about groups and their potential. My attitudes toward groups have changed, and I see the small group as having much more potentiality for communication than I had realized."

"Analyzing group processes is tied to understanding and loving people."

"It began to depend far more on the discussion as to who were the participants or nonparticipants. People began to assume new roles and far less consistent roles."

"I would recommend that, in the future, it would be profitable for the professor to delineate a definite structure for the group at the beginning of the quarter. . . . (It) is a mistake to think that undergraduates will ever do anything by themselves unless they really become enthusiastic about it."

"I believe that the seminar gave me more confidence and furthered my ability to make the group move in the direction that I desired."

". . . leadership is most effective when it is shared, when it is not self-conscious, and when others are not particularly conscious of it. Effective leadership requires and inspires self-confidence; it cannot be used to prove and illustrate to oneself and to others one's own capabilities, although it may have that effect."

"An effective leader . . . can use his energy to help others contribute in the most effective manner and to create an atmosphere in which the other members will be willing to assume a part of his role—which he must be willing to relinquish."

"I think that more theoretical knowledge on my part would have upgraded the quality of my observations considerably."

"I think there should be more structure, in terms of leadership, from the leader. This could be done by having *required* readings and some academic work, centering, for example, on 'The Group Member' one week and 'Consensus Achieving' another. I know these suggestions imply quite a bit of structure, but I think this is not only my desire, but the desire of a number of other group members."

"Now I find myself withholding judgment until I get to know people better."

The student evaluations indicate some measure of growth and understanding in this interdisciplinary area. Evidently the experience served to introduce students to the dynamics of small-group functioning and helped them to become more aware of the interactive behavior of group members. As our Self-descriptive Questionnaire also indicates, student self-evaluations reveal generally positive changes in communication, group relations, and in skills of observation and participation. The statistical results are reported here in Part III, entitled Research and Evaluation.

The group-centered approach permitted student involvement in the planning and carrying out of the workshop design and process. The opportunity to "learn by doing" in immediate group situations combined both theory and practice and encouraged total participation in the ongoing learning process.

A longer time period that might be found in other settings would allow more latitude and variability in both content and practice than was available in our current calendar. Nevertheless, Antioch's experience with this component suggests that teachers of speech, for instance, might very well expand their courses in Public Speaking or Group Discussion in the directions indicated here. This would serve to increase the viability of current speech courses and augment the interdisciplinary efforts being initiated in many college and university curricula.

Interpersonal Communication

Definitions and Derivations

The study of interpersonal communication owes some debt to group social work, speech discussion, counseling groups, and, more importantly, to the "sensitivity" and "training" groups of the National Training Laboratories Institute for Applied Behavioral Science. The T-group approach to teaching and learning has been a formalized part of Human Relations Training for some time, where it is used to heighten self-awareness and the skills of interactive behavior. In this training, increased communicative skill appeared to be a natural outcome of increased interpersonal effectiveness. So it seemed particularly justifiable to incorporate this methodology as a component in a viable communication program.

At a Conference on Communication Skills and Interpersonal Relations held at Antioch, Dr. Norman Paris summarized the goals and processes of the NTL T-groups:

Generally the broad overall goals of a laboratory training experience are to learn in a small-group situation as much as one can and wants to learn in the areas of:

Heightened understanding of self and ability for productive self-insight (perceived self-concept, ideal self-concept, assumptions about others' perception of self).

Heightened understanding of others (perceptions of others, the generalized other, and specific individuals and groups).

Enriched modes of experiencing and responding with increased interpersonal effectiveness

A T-group consists of eight or twelve participants and one or two trainers. There is usually no agenda and no predetermined task or activity beyond the implicit expectation to learn about oneself and others. There is a focus on the "here and now." The trainer does not play the part of traditional group leader, although he frequently will participate in the group as a function of his own or the group's needs, as he sees his behavior helping in the group's development.

In a very real sense the beginning of such a group represents the formation of a new society. It is a group that has no traditions or norms, the decision-making apparatus is unclear, and the only commitment is to learn as much as one can. There are several additional underlying goals or meta-goals implicit in a laboratory:

The goal of expanded consciousness and recognition of choice; the "givens" or "assumed" become options.

The goal of developing a spirit of inquiry within a climate of responsible freedom and of increasing openness and honesty.

The goal of developing a collaborative pattern of leadership and an expanded conception of the role and the person in an authority or leadership position.

The goal of developing an increased capacity for establishing "authentic relationships"; interactions where all parties are enhanced and none are put down or lessened by the experience.

Finally, it is important to emphasize again the basic working principle of training groups—that, by and large, the group generates its own data instead of having an expert deliver lectures on how groups develop and function or on the psychodynamics of interpersonal relationships. By working in the "here and now," the group can see for itself its own functioning and its own development; individuals can observe the impact they have on others and develop new skills for giving and receiving feedback, for exercising leadership functions, and for participating in helping relationships.

The initiation of the experimental first-year program at Antioch permitted a nontraditional approach for our interpersonal-communication component. We did not need to be concerned with traditional subject matter or traditional teaching and evaluation. Our concerns, rather, were in attracting interested and motivated students, keeping to a workable number of participants, creating a group-centered structure, and creating a climate of inquiry and trust on a behavioral, here-and-now level.

Our syllabus briefly stated the purpose of "interpersonal communication":

To increase personal effectiveness and competence through the intellectual and emotional understanding of interpersonal, individual, and group behavior, the class will focus on the personal growth of the student in self-awareness, confidence in self-expression, greater perceptivity, and sensitivity to the feelings and expressions of others.

Procedure:

The group interaction provides the learning data that inform each individual about his impact on others. The group affords the experimental setting where new behaviors and relationships can be attempted. Readings, discussion, and group exercises provide the milieu for these basic learning encounters, which are termed "T-groups" or sensitivity training groups.

At the initial meeting, the instructor explained the objectives and the procedures of this course section—called variously Workshop, Seminar, and Laboratory. The purpose was explained, a reading list of books on interpersonal relationships and self-understanding was recommended, the use of the video recording was demonstrated, and the experimental nature of the program was made clear, which, in turn, justified the administration of personality, interaction, and other pre- and post-tests. After the voluntary nature of student participation was made plain, a few expectations were enumerated.

Students were to agree to attend regularly, participate as fully as they were able, read in the recommended bibliography as far as their interest and time permitted, maintain a written personal log of their reactions, and submit the log for weekly comments from the instructor. The Interpersonal Communication "Laboratory" was under way.

As the workshop evolved over its three-year period, the inter-personal-communication component grew from ten weeks of two periods of one and one-half hours to longer periods of two and one-half to three hours each, plus the playback time of video recording review. Over this time, the groups averaged between sixteen and eighteen participants, including both freshmen and upperclassmen. The group met in a newly furbished television studio and sat semi-nar-fashion around movable tables, with microphones and television cameras exposed to view. Typically, as the meetings progressed and group action intensified, the formal table-and-chair setting gave way to more comfortable and less formal arrangements—yet still within range of the microphones and cameras. The "labs" were group-centered, generally unstructured, and informal at the start—allowing first names to be used. A coffee break of fifteen or twenty minutes permitted social interactions at yet another communication level.

In the beginning, after the initial remarks by the instructor-trainer and after a period of uneasy silence, some of the more vocal students can be expected to question or protest an approach that leaves the group without observable direction or procedure. Often, in the first meetings, the instructor is assailed for abdicating his traditional role as leader and planner for the group. This openly expressed resentment provides opportunity to deal with authority and dependency problems and to ventilate the strong feelings accompanying child-parent, student-teacher, employee-employer relationships.

Any underlying problems in the formation or composition of

the group will generally appear spontaneously—for example, residual feelings about the course if it is a requirement; obvious segregations such as graduate vs. undergraduate students, black vs. white students, field majors vs. general education students, teachers vs. administrators, males vs. females. Tension derived from these diversifications requires early attention by the group.

The instructor-trainer must be prepared for group flight from the here-and-now toward intellectualizations that avoid or deny feelings and the necessary confrontations with difficult issues. Sometimes, merely pointing this out to the group moves the discussion out of its tangential orbit. It is helpful when the instructor-trainer can serve as a "model learner" who is aware of his own feelings, sensitive to the feelings of others, and open enough to express them to the group as they spontaneously occur.

The instructor-trainer does not abdicate but is just not playing a traditional authoritarian role. He is most certainly present in an emotional sense and, in those terms, is an influential member of the group. What is abdicated is the expectation that the instructor-trainer be responsible for the structuring, for the learning, and for the success of the group. He rarely structures; he is not responsible for the group's learning or for the success of the group. The group, in fact, may benefit immensely by becoming bogged down and dishearteningly immobilized. It then becomes the group's task to mobilize itself back into effective functioning. This eventuality provides the group with a sense of accomplishment and confidence that could not be mustered if the instructor-trainer had "saved" the group by some superimposed technique. It was Richard Farson, Director of the Western Behavioral Sciences Institute, who stated in an unpublished paper that an initial failure effectively mobilizes untapped resources of a group or an individual and leads frequently to creative accomplishment.[2]

Participants come to realize that they are less unique and more like one another than they had previously supposed. They find that getting close to other human beings is infinitely rewarding, even if fraught with initial apprehensiveness. They discover resiliencies within themselves that they had not previously recognized.

---

[2]Paper read at the American Psychological Association Annual meeting, New York, 1966.

They discover tendernesses within that they had mistaken for vulnerability. But before tender and compassionate feelings are revealed, the group members must develop a feeling of trust in one another—and this requires the shattering of the common fear that open and honest groups are basically hostile and that weaknesses and inadequacies will be ridiculed. "Feedback" is generally more than fair, and supportive as well; however, arrogance or indifference will not be handled as gently. Once weaknesses are shown and accepted, fragility diminishes and more creative risk-taking can be attempted. In this atmosphere the shy, the hesitant, and the reserved can come forward, and communication can be enhanced for all participants.

The group need not be abandoned entirely to its own devices. There are times when more structured interventions can enhance communication, highlight undercurrents of conflict, or deepen perception. Occasionally, these interactive experiences were initiated by the instructor-trainer to facilitate learning by experience. Some of the nonverbal experiences were intended to heighten awareness of expressive movements and gestures as significant communication.

While "mirroring," for example, a student pair would follow each other's hand or body movements to music or to other rhythmic patterns in order to heighten empathetic responses. The entire group is divided up into pairs for this "echoing" or "mirroring" exercise.

The degree of trust a member may feel toward the group might be experienced in a practice exercise by the "supporting circle," where the standing group closely surrounds a single member, who allows himself to "fall" as his fellows pass him gently from hand to hand. A physical confirmation of collective support can be experienced by a member as the group elevates and gently rocks him in a horizontal position. More aggressive feelings are released when the group stands in a circle and excludes a single member who must physically force his way into the resisting group. Feelings of exclusion, isolation, and aggressiveness are generated and resolved by this exercise. Other nonverbal exercises can be found in the book by Malamud and in a more recent book by Schutz (see Bibliography).

In another type of exercise, stereotyping and perception are both involved as the group speculates on the personality characteristics of each member from sketches of a person he had drawn previously and anonymously. The lessons learned are that symbolic representations comprise an extension of the personality and very often reveal attitudes and feelings toward the self, and that this perceptiveness can be enhanced with practice.

Sociograms provide members with feedback about their positions in the group and in others' perceptions of them. Some useful feedback questions are to ask the name of the person they would like to follow, the person they would seek out to discuss a personal problem, and the one they would prefer as a friend. When these are compiled and diagramed, they give the members helpful data to consider and discuss.

Subgroupings are also valuable when more intensive participation and interaction is desired. A smaller group interacting while seated within the large group will provide data that the observing group can later share with the participants in the small "inner" group. "Triads" provide an opportunity for those who are more reserved to participate more fully and more intimately than they are free to do at first in the larger group. In this exercise, groups of three students separate themselves around the room and carry out some proscribed task requiring agreement among them; or two of them may give the third member a feedback about their initial or current perceptions of him. The recipient of the feedback is required to remain silent for about five minutes, after which he is permitted to respond. Then another member of the triad is singled out for feedback, until all three have had the experience of hearing themselves discussed openly by two other people. A common reaction is surprise about how kind and gentle people are when much more critical data were anticipated. The three emerge closer and friendlier than before.

An "alter ego" exercise tests empathy and perception while stimulating more open and honest expression. During this exercise, a member will stand behind another, interrupt, and speak out for the other what he infers are the honest thoughts and feelings of that individual. The individual is free to deny or admit the accuracy of what his alter ego asserts as his "real feelings." In this way, group members become more receptive to their own internal sensorium and are aided by example in expressing their more open and honest responses. They become, in Carl Rogers sense, more "congruent."

When a member requests open feedback from the entire group, he dons the "invisible mantle" which allows the group to discuss him as if he were not present. The member most often learns that groups are supportive rather than punitive, and that he is much more acceptable to others—with all his faults—than he had dared to hope.

The videotape recording provided additional feedback in a more telling, if a less subjective, way. The impact of self-confrontation through these recordings is discussed elsewhere in detail, but it can be noted here that the television camera and screen are excellent teaching-learning tools in this setting. Because television provides immediate, complete feedback that is impartial, objective, and direct, it is both valuable and humbling for all who expose themselves to its view. Although not essential to laboratories of this kind, our program has been most fortunate in having this valuable educational tool.

Toward the close of the Laboratory in Interpersonal Communication, data from the pre- and post-tests provided evidence of individual changes and afforded an opportunity to discuss the accuracy of perceptions of self and others. The Self-descriptive Questionnaire, the Leary "Interpersonal Checklist, the Schutz "Fundamental Interpersonal Relations Orientation", the Edwards "Personality Preference Schedule", and the Q-sort (see section on Research and Evaluation) all furnished individualized data which aided in more accurate self-perceptions.

As authentic and accepting relationships grow, creative risks become more possible so that defensiveness diminishes and self-esteem is enhanced. Under these conditions, meaningful communication can occur openly, honestly, and with surprising directness. The exercises are seen as techniques to facilitate this interaction and this communication. The entire experience also encourages intra-communication within the participant, who is helped to sense a wider range of feelings and to rely more consistently upon his own reactions and response. This experience allows each member to reassess his own potential and his competencies, which, in turn, leads to experimentation and change in behavior and the learning of new interactive skills.

The following excerpts from student evaluations indicate their subjective assessment of the experience and the changes they perceived in their attitudes and behavior:

"There comes a point now when I cannot possibly react differently than I do, and I do not have to worry about doubting my reactions and responses, for the self cannot be wrong; it cannot be bad."

"Before this quarter, I evaluated myself almost entirely on what I heard from others about myself. Whatever I heard, I tried to live up to because I didn't really believe it and I had to prove it to myself. It's really strange, but I have found that people have been pretty wrong about me."

"Sharing my weaknesses now, instead of merely proffering my ideas and strengths, is important to me—I discovered I was not fragile."

"As much as I am able to view my own progress communicatively and interpersonally, I feel that as a result of the situations and confrontations of the group meetings I have become much more open to people in general and much more open and honest (the honesty that comes with more self-knowledge) with myself."

"Perhaps the most significant realization I have made is that I do have ideas that are worth and need expression, that I can take a rational and a leading role and that I have a need for this kind of importance."

"I didn't quite realize what a personal thing communication really is. We did not study, practice, and perfect a casual skill. Communication was treated, not as a handy tool toward achieving nonrelated goals, the organization of a group project, or the transfer of an idea, but rather as a way of knowing and reaching the real in people, oneself and others."

"I cannot dismiss the communication seminar lightly. There was a point near the beginning when I was delightedly discovering things: that light conversation might have very different and very important underlying messages . . . that there was a wide range of possibilities for communication and human contact, verbal, visual, tactile, intuitive. I have not lost all this."

"I am less afraid to make a mistake or expose myself. And as a result, I can *listen* to other people with more of me. I am not as concerned with guarding myself as I have been."

"As the workshop progressed and I found myself becoming deeply involved in other people's fears and desires, I began feeling more and more a sense of responsibility for myself and the entire group."

"It would be my estimation that whenever learning occurs on the T-group type level, with feelings and personal involvement, it is much more meaningful than by traditional lecture or reading techniques."

"I have learned the trick of understanding others and their troubles by looking for the same feelings in myself."

"The class made me curious about human nature. Why do people act in certain ways in certain situations? Why do some people have tremendous defenses up? Are defenses necessarily bad? Which are 'good'? . . . How do different people react to the same situation? Why?"

"I did learn one important thing about myself: I was looking at the world through mother-colored glasses, so that the scope of my reactions was limited."

"I feel a little like a client in Carl Rogers' book going through therapy."

"We all seek self-understanding in an almost frantic, desperate way . . . now I realize that the answer to my existence lies within me."

"The messages that communication is important, that words are not the only carriers of meaning, that the human interactions under even the most trivial words are important, and that for effective communication and full understanding, openness, awareness, and willingness to listen are necessary—all came through in the presentations."

"Those in the group who felt 'alone' with their problems realized that others shared or had the same problems."

"From this seminar I've realized a desire—a desire to help others and to accept help, and a sort of amazement at the world of feelings—a world I have hid from."

"I have learned the difference between 'psyching out' people and trying to understand them."

" . . . we grew together and helped each other grow."

As the evaluations indicate, the utilization of T-groups, sensitivity training, or the "human relations" approach can be a highly successful, if unconventional, learning experience for students in the direction of greater self-understanding, confidence in self-expression, and in interactive skills. The experience does provide both practice and growth in communicative skills, which depend, in turn, upon many psychodynamic factors frequently neglected in traditional skill courses.

Part II

DESIGN AND OPERATION OF THE
VIDEOTAPE RECORDING FACILITY

T HE RECORDING STUDIO used in the program was a seminar room modified by the addition of four television cameras mounted at shoulder height in the corners, and five microphones mounted on stands bolted to the ceiling. Each camera and motorized 10:1 zoom lens was mounted on a mechanical pan and tilt unit. The room also contained a 23-inch viewing monitor and a custom-built remote unit to control the videotape recorder and the viewing monitor. A minimal increase in lighting enhanced the room's televising capabilities, while at the same time retaining a normal degree of classroom lighting.

All of the equipment in the studio was designed to be manipulated, directed, and monitored completely from a control room located on the same floor but at the opposite end of the building. No technical personnel were present in the classroom. The control room housed a monitor and electronic control unit for each camera, a mechanical control unit for panning, tilting, zooming, and focusing each camera and lens, an Ampex 660-B videotape recorder, audio equipment, a library of videotapes, and spare parts and maintenance equipment. A two-channel switcher-fader unit and a line monitor gave the facility on-line editing capabilities.

Additions were later made to both the control room and the studio. Beige draperies were hung in the studio classroom to improve the quality of audio and video. A kinescope film recorder made possible the production of film from existing videotapes and a portable video recording unit provided greater flexibility in remote field recording. During the first two years of operation, supplementary equipment, such as microphones and coaxial cable, was added as needed.

Operation of Equipment

The remote-control system was designed so that recording or playback of videotapes could be initiated from either the studio classroom or the control room. Although tape-threading, camera movement, selection, and signal monitoring had to be done in the control room, the process could be started, via the remote-control unit, by the instructor or group in the studio classroom. One switch on this control unit turned the classroom monitor on and off. Another switch opened an intercom audio channel to the control room, allowing the classroom instructor to converse with the control-room personnel. The unit also contained a plug for a two-way telephone headset. A five-position joystick on the control unit engaged the videotape recorder for playback, record, a fast-forward, a rewind, and a neutral position. This control unit provided the classroom instructor or leader with the option of structuring the playback session. The tape could be started or stopped as desired, skimmed through using the fast-forward position, or reviewed as many times as desired using the rewind position. This type of remote control lent itself to flexible review and discussion of videotapes under various feedback designs. The videotape could thus be used as a feedback resource that did not dictate structure. This left the instructor and group free to manipulate the data by the stopping, replaying, selecting, and sequencing of incidents. This is in contrast, for example, to Nielsen, who found that his confrontation sessions were rigidly structured by the amount of film held by the movie camera.[a]

One of the major considerations in designing the facility was simplicity of operation and maintenance. All taping operations could be conducted by students. Several students were hired quarterly to assist in the taping program and in short time could successfully conduct the entire taping operation.

Use of Videotaping in the Communication Program

The success of projects utilizing videotape as a feedback mechanism, combined with a general knowledge of its potential, indicated to us that the structured use of videotape as a teacher-tool in our communication workshop could strengthen some of the most important elements of this "encounter group." The capability of remotely controlling the television equipment allowed us to video-

---

[a]Nielsen, Gerhard: *Studies in Self-Confrontation.* Cleveland, Howard Allen, 1964.

tape workshop groups without placing conspicuous people and cumbersome equipment in the classroom. The minor alterations of the room did not make it significantly different from a standard classroom. The flexibility afforded by our remote-control unit and the in-class monitor allowed for a variety of playback possibilities. The economy of a student-staffed operation and reusable tapes allowed extensive utilization of the videotape equipment. Our initial efforts were aimed at exploring the diverse potentials that the immediacy of television could afford.

The design of the program permitted a variety of activities with videotape recording and viewing. Groups were scheduled to meet in the studio classroom twice weekly; one session was concerned with speaking and listening skills, and the other was devoted to the understanding of group processes. All meetings were videotaped. While several different videotaping designs were used at first, the one reported below has appeared most effective and efficient in serving the ends of the workshop, without imposing technical limitations.

The playback session was seen as the most important function of the videotaping process. During the laboratory period, the individual is presented with certain stimuli to which he actively responds; he cannot objectively observe the dynamics of interaction because he is involved in those dynamics. Playbacks were seen, in this light, as informal periods of observation, confrontation, and discussion. In addition to initiating self-confrontation, the playback sessions, it was hoped, would also stimulate a growing awareness of, and an analytical approach toward, group process and group functioning.

Three types of playback sessions were used: the regularly scheduled review session, the spontaneous immediate playback, and the more carefully selected total-quarter review session. Regularly scheduled review sessions were most frequent. The other two playback designs were used intermittently when workshop members felt them necessary or desirable.

The playbacks were optional and were scheduled three times weekly in convenient time blocks. Each student was usually *able* to attend one or more of the three sessions. Further, a single student or group of students could request additional playback time if both the facility, personnel operators, and staff members were available. In this way, students were given ample opportunity to view the playbacks and discuss them as many times as desired.

Although a member of the teaching team was usually present during playbacks, the review sessions were generally informal, unstructured, and nondirective. Group members present at the playback could request to see any portions of the tapes from the previous class meeting. Through use of the remote-control unit, students and members of the teaching team had the option of viewing, in depth, any portion of the recorded tapes. The focused feedback technique of more precise selection of incident might be equally effective in this context.[4] The focused technique was used more consistently in structuring the total-quarter review sessions.

The existence of group pressure encouraged attendance at playback sessions. In most instances, playback time accounted for about 50 per cent of the total workshop involvement. Some participants attended all of the three weekly playbacks; seldom did any group member *miss* all three playbacks. This pressure existed despite the fact that attendance at playbacks was optional. One possible explanation for this pressure may lie in the depth of involvement felt by students in "reliving" the workshop experience; an interaction experience, which was initally involving, is reconstructed in its entirety on videotape from another involving perspective—that of observer.

Late in the program, in keeping with a shift from self-attention to group attention, the central activity at playback sessions turned from viewing to discussion. Rather than perfunctorily attempting to review the entire set of tapes from the previous class meeting, the students spent the playback time attempting to discern, clarify, and discuss specific points of process. In these later sessions, five or ten minutes of videotape viewing often served as the basis for several hours of group discussion.

Student Response

Students were at first very wary of the television equipment and the videotape recording situation, and expressed the general feeling

---

[4]Stoller, Frederick H.: The use of focused feedback via videotape in small groups. *Explorations in Human Relations Training*. Washington, D.C., National Training Laboratories, National Education Association, 1966.

that "someone is back there watching me . . . ." Visiting the control room, watching and talking to the operator, and discussing the reasons for using the equipment seemed to generate some measure of trust and understanding. The workshop members usually came to look upon the cameramen as a part of the group and were more at ease in the recording situation.

The initial impact of the equipment was superseded by the initial experiences of self-confrontation. Most workshop participants were taken aback, embarrassed, amused, or generally uncomfortable. Students were first of all interested in manifest behavior, directing their attention to physical appearances and behaviors:

> "I hated myself—thought I looked and sounded awful and said inane things."
> "I can remember the first session quite well. I felt utterly phoney and a bit 'too smart for my own breeches.' Suffice it to say that I couldn't stand to look at myself on the television (something which I can still do without). . . ."

Later, the workshop members began to explore the third-person objectivity which the tapes afforded:

> "It is an unusual experience to be able to gain a little distance by being able to watch oneself. . . ."

The result of such objective confrontation at the playback sessions was usually a discussion between students of what they were *really* trying to project, the feelings they thought they had expressed verbally or nonverbally, the contrast in the videotape image, and the individual's self-image, the responses and reactions elicited, and the ways in which the individual might or might not have been more effective and/or responsive.

> ". . . through videotaping in the group, I became aware of how often I don't finish sentences and how I sound when I'm fairly incoherent."

The concern for the individual's self-image and behavior was tempered by an increasing concern for the group, group process, and the individual's role as a functioning member of the group. One student reported:

> "Not only do I see more about others and myself at the playback, but I also see more about the group as a whole unit. I see it grow and develop week after week. . . . This is more noticeable to me during the playbacks."

The students felt that they missed many things as they originally happened—subtleties of group process, reactions, responses, nonverbal cues and messages and, in general, things that happened out of the range of observers' perceptions at the time of the meeting. One student mentioned in his log that a particular role-play

". . . was a blur to me at the time it was going on . . . I didn't get much out of it . . . until I saw the videotape. . . .'"

Another mentioned that

". . . much more of what actually happened can be seen from the neutral position of sitting back and watching the tapes."

Students often became interested in the expressive physical movements of the group interaction, spending parts of playback sessions viewing the tape without sound and then speculating on the impact and meaning of what they saw before the tape was replayed *with* sound. Workshop members were often amazed at the fact that physical movement could do so much to enhance, supplement, distort, negate, or neutralize the meanings of verbal communication. In one case a student, while attempting to tell the group that a particular issue "didn't really matter," was quite taken aback by the conspicuous tension in his clenched fists, wrinkled forehead, and hunched posture. In the playback session, other workshop members were quick to point out to him that "it really did matter!"

Evaluations and student logs have indicated generally high acceptance of videotape in the workshop. The initial feelings of wariness and apprehension about the taping process, and the anxiety inherent in initial experiences with self-confrontation, were replaced by an acceptance of the videotape as an important and useful source of objective feedback. Reflecting upon his experience, one student wrote in his final log:

"It's strange now to think back to the beginning. . . . We were all so conscious of the cameras and now we hardly know that they are there. They may have held up progress at the beginning, but in the long run they were one of the most important factors in our development."

Gerhard Nielsen put it very succinctly when he said of his experiences with media-initiated self-confrontation, "The confrontation with the self-image left none of them neutral or untouched. . . ."[5]

Immediate and Elapsed-time Playbacks

Although it has not been used extensively, the immediate playback in the classroom of a critical incident presents a somewhat dif-

---

[5]Nielsen, Gerhard: *Studies in Self-Confrontation.* Cleveland, Howard Allen, 1964.

ferent form of confrontation and/or process analysis. While the group is still meeting and is still relatively close to the situation in question, the videotape can be replayed and the group can immediately view what has just taken place. This immediate replay is an additional source of data on individual behavior and group functioning otherwise not available.

The videotape was also used to review a series of meetings to provide data on individual and group changes over a long period of time. The instructors first selected segments of tapes drawn from the entire course of the workshop, chosen to illustrate representative issues, problems, and positive or negative changes in group and individual behavior. A program of these segments was drawn up and run in sequence for the whole group. In these elapsed-time playbacks, the feedback tended to be more directed. Rather than just providing an overview of group development, the tapes acted as a catalyst in generating further group discussion and interaction.

Additional Uses of Videotape

The speech section of the workshop in communication and interpersonal relations also utilized videotape as a feedback device. Recordings of prose and poetry readings, and of conversational speech, by each student were made at the beginning and at the end of the workshop, and these recordings were compared to indicate growth and change. Recordings were also made of the demonstration speeches, persuasive speeches, dramatic and poetic readings, and extemporaneous speaking. The advantage of replaying videotape in a speech program was obvious: The objective feedback provided by the tape gave students a picture of how they "came across" in various speech activities. Students had the opportunity to respond to themselves as others respond to their various speaking and reading presentations. Students with distracting speech mannerisms were provided with close-up views and could study the movements involved in producing particular distractions. Poise and greater skill in speech delivery were better served through the feedback provided by videotape.

Instructors and staff also made use of the videotaped material for improving their own methods of teaching group skills and for sharpening their diagnostic abilities. Edited videotape clips highlighted individual and group behavioral changes, and were available for continued training activities. The 16-mm film referred to previously will use such clips as indication of the videotape resource and of the changes that can be anticipated.

Finally, we are now experimenting with the use of videotape as a research and reporting device. The addition of a kinescope film recorder to our facility permits production of filmed reports on the project and the development of teaching materials drawn either from unrehearsed group activities or from isolated and edited "critical incidents" illustrative of various issues, problems, and modes of group and individual interactions and behaviors.

Part III

RESEARCH AND EVALUATION

THIS SECTION CONTAINS an overview of our research approaches during the seven quarters that the workshop has been offered. The planning group hypothesized that participation in a communications course should bring about measurable or observable changes in self-expression, self-confidence, and openness in speaking situations—in brief, more sensitive communication. Subsumed here would be less defensiveness, greater ease of participation, a more realistic self-appraisal, and a wider range of emotional expression and receptivity. This is not dissimilar to research results found in those participating in T-group encounters.[6] It appeared to us that changes in participation and communicative relationships would follow positive changes in the concept of self or self-image. For this reason, a number of personality scales and self-perceived change measures were used in addition to the audiotape and videotape recordings of observable changes.

Since the inception of the program, the rating scales, questionnaires, and interaction indices which were tried included the Edwards "Personality Preference Schedule," the Leary "Interpersonal Checklist and Personality Wheel," the Schutz "Fundamental Interpersonal Relations Orientation (FIRO-B)," and some locally compiled Q-sorts and questionnaires.

During the first year of the workshop, each student was asked to fill out a Background Information Form covering speaking, interpersonal relations, and group skills. The student was asked his reasons for enrolling, his previous speech and communication experiences, and the specific speaking skills he wished to improve. He was asked to specify the interpersonal skills he wished to learn or improve and, finally, his personal reactions to speaking situations. This information was helpful in assessing the student's own

---

[6]Stock, Dorothy: A survey of research on T-groups. In Bradford, L.; Gibb, J., and Beene, K. (Eds.): *T-Group Theory and Laboratory Method*. New York; Wiley, 1964, p. 424.

perceptions of his needs and interests, in planning the program, and in reviewing accomplishments later in the term. It was later discontinued when more useful measures were introduced.

The first pre- and post-test administered on an experimental basis was the FIRO-B, measuring three basic constructs—inclusion, control, and affection—which Schutz bases on a three-dimensional theory of interpersonal behavior. Each construct is broken down into two dimensions of "wanted" and "expressed" needs. Over a period of three quarters, the test was administered to five groups beginning with two groups in the fall of 1965; there were thirteen members in each group. A t-test of significance-of-differences between the means showed no change in one group and a significant difference at the .01 level for the other group on the "Control Wanted" variable. In the same group, at the .05 level, a significant difference was found between pre-test and post-test scores for males in the categories of "Affection Expressed" and "Affection Wanted."

In the winter of 1966, one group emerged significantly on the Affection Wanted variable and the other group on the Control Wanted variable—both at the .05 level of significance. Again, in the spring of 1966, a similar significant difference was found for females in the Control Wanted category.

The results of the FIRO-B were not conclusive but did indicate some changes in self-perception as students became more aware and more accepting of their interactive needs and wishes. Evidently, a short course in communication does not make sweeping changes in attitudes or behavior but rather increases awareness of needs as trust and openness develop within the group. It was interesting to note the recurrence of the Control Wanted variable in three separate groups. This may reflect a growing anxiousness with the unstructured and permissive group climate rather than any deeper personality needs. Both males and females expressed more need for affection in both the wanted (passive) and expressed (active) mode. It may also be inferred that students at the college age are struggling with conflicts around dependence-independence, both wishing for, and denying needs for, external control over their feelings and behavior.

The Edwards Personality Preference Schedule is a forced-choice personality test constructed from Murray's "need" variables that measure achievement, deference, orderliness, exhibition, autonomy, affiliation, intraception, succorance, dominance, abasement, nurturance, change, endurance, heterosexuality, and aggression.

The schedule was administered during the winter and spring of 1966 with the expectation of measuring changes in the students' self-concepts after taking the course. Three groups were given pre- and post-tests, and then a t-test of differences was obtained at the .05 level of significance and better. The group served as its own control. In the winter, both groups showed the following changes: "affiliation" increased for males; "dominance" increased for females; "deference" decreased for females; "endurance" decreased for females; "intraception" increased for females.

"Affiliation" is defined as loyalty to friends, participation in groups, forming new friendships. "Dominance" is defined as the willingness to argue for one's point of view, to be a leader in groups, to persuade and influence others to do what one wants. "Deference" is defined as the tendency to get suggestions from others, to find out what others think, to follow instructions, and do what is expected. "Endurance" is the tendency to keep at a job until it is finished; to work hard, and to stick at a problem. "Intraception" is defined as the tendency to analyze one's motives and feelings, to observe others, to understand how others feel about problems, to put oneself in another's place, to analyze the behavior of others.

Of the single group tested in the spring, "autonomy" increased while "deference" decreased for females; "affiliation" increased for males; "change" decreased for males; and "heterosexuality" increased for females.

"Autonomy" is to say what one thinks, to be independent when making decisions, to do things without regard to what others might say. "Change" is defined as the tendency to do new and different things, to welcome novelty. "Heterosexuality" is interest in the opposite sex.

Most of the changes were found among the females in all of the groups tested. "Change" and "affiliation" were the only significant variables for the males. It may be that females are more amenable to change of attitude and behavior during the college years when placed in settings which facilitate open interchange—or it may be that, like "Thursday's child," the females have a longer way to go in breaking away from cultural patterns or socialization expectations and restrictions.

It is not unexpected that "affiliation" should increase after a course of this kind. That this increase was confined to males suggests that they found less need to assert their independence than they did on the pre-test but developed closer personal relationships that they were willing to acknowledge by the end of the workshop. That the females were free to behave with more "dominance" and "autonomy" and less "deference" suggests less dependence upon culturally derived patterns of behavior.

The differences in "endurance" and in "heterosexuality"—one decreasing and the latter increasing—again suggest that the females were relinquishing an expected competitive role for a more primary one that could move more easily in the direction of self-fulfillment.

The absence of a control group and the small population under test mitigate against further generalizations from our results with the Edwards Personality Preference Schedule. Nevertheless, the fact that changes did occur with some regularity and in similar directions indicates a degree of support for the assumption that needs and attitudes toward the self and others change with interactive experiences which encourage deeper and more honest communicative attempts.

A Q-sort of seventy-three statements was used in a test-retest pattern during the fall and winter of the academic year 1966-67. Some statements were compiled from earlier student evaluations of their own self-perceived changes after completing the workshop, while others were modified from statements found in the Edwards Personality Preference Schedule, the Omnibus Personality Inventory, and the Bell Adjustment Inventory. The items focus on self-concepts, attitudes about group participation, interactive behavior, and aspects of communication. The seventy-three statements presented in Appendix C, were each typed on a separate card, and all participating students were given a set of the cards and were instructed as follows:

> You are to sort these cards into 7 groups according to the following criteria: For the first grouping, choose the 4 items that are most characteristic or descriptive of your behavior and attitudes. In the second group, put the 7 cards that are very descriptive of you, but not of the first rank. In the third group, put the 15 next most descriptive items; in the fourth, 21 cards; in the fifth, 15 cards;

in the sixth, 7 cards; and in the last group, the 4 cards that are least descriptive of you.

The students were given answer sheets divided into the seven groups, creating a forced-choice pattern. In the fall, the experimental group numbered thirty-three and the control group numbered fifteen. In the winter workshop, there were twenty-two experimental students who completed both the pre- and post-tests. There was no control group in the winter quarter.

To ascertain direction of change for each item, we used McNemar's test for changes as given in Siegel's publication.[7] Students had changed on twenty-nine items in the post-test by more than eight each of the experimental subjects. These items were numbers 1, 3, 6, 7, 11, 16, 17, 18, 20, 21, 24, 25, 26, 34, 37, 38, 40, 42, 47, 48, 52, 53, 56, 60, 61, 65, 68, 71, 73. The two items below showed significant changes:

40. I tend to stutter or become inarticulate when speaking before groups (less like self). (P < .01).
49. I prefer a structured situation with clear goals and assigned tasks (more like self). (P < .05).

The absolute amounts of change in the experimental group when compared with the control group were as follows:

E-group 21% of change overall; 30% change per item
C-group 18% of change overall; 23% change per item

The Q-sort indicated little change of significance in the experimental group. This may reflect upon the validity of the testing measure itself, which had not been standardized with any normative data. More tests of the instrument need to be made to validate its usefulness for the purposes and populations it was designed to measure. Students, nevertheless, did see themselves as more articulate at the time of the post-test, with perhaps some impatience at the free-wheeling, unstructured setting in which they found themselves.

In a very limited way, the Leary Interpersonal Checklist and Personality Wheel were used in a pilot study of the instruments during the winter of 1968.[8] Only six subjects completed the pre-

---

[7]Siegel, Sidney: *Non-Parametric Statistics for the Behavioral Sciences.* New York; McGraw, 1956.

[8]Leary, Timothy: The theory and measurement of interpersonal communication. In Bennis, W. *et al.: The Planning of Change.* New York, Holt, 1961.

and post-test questionnaire. The checklist consists of 128 items describing attitudes and behavior in human interaction. The student is first asked to select items descriptive of his "real self." He then selects items that describe his "ideal self." This is a variation of Leary's suggested use, as he uses the checklist to compare self-ratings with ratings of others. We used self-ratings only.

The Personality Wheel is arranged in the form of a sixteen-point circular grid that reflects a variety of interpersonal purposes and behaviors. Some of the categories are "modest-self-effacing," "managerial-autocratic," "competitive-exploitative," and "docile-dependent." Raw scores from real self and ideal self are converted to locations on the wheel. The amount of difference between those points at the beginning of the term is compared to the amount of difference at the end of the test period.

In five out of the six cases, the difference between the real-self and the ideal-self had diminished by the second test. In another setting, with a larger number of subjects, the writer found similar results when applying this measure in a human relations course at the University of Kansas. The approximation of the two "selves" in these pilot studies suggests that this instrument might be the most useful, to date, of all the measures attempted in evaluating the effects of a course in interpersonal communication. If statistically verified, the approximation might indicate a greater self-acceptance, although one might speculate if the direction of change indicated that the subjects found more realistic self-images, abandoned unrealistic goals for themselves, or found themselves more acceptable as they were. Additional research using this instrument, with a larger population, a control group, and more exacting experimental conditions is indicated.

Burke and Bennis,[9] in their study of changes of perception of self and others, used a Group Semantic Differential Test, which uses bipolar ratings for concept-scale pairings on a seven-point continuum. Their concepts were "The way I actually am in the T-group," "The way I would like to be," and "The way I see others." They found that group members became more satisfied with their perceptions of themselves, became more like their actual self-

[9]Burke, R. L., and Bennis, W. G.: Changes in perception of self and others during human relations training. *Human Relations, XIV*:165-179, May 1961.

percepts in the direction of their ideal, and became more congruent in their perceptions of others.

Another instrument which provided more useful data in our program was administered in the winter quarter of 1968 with a group of twenty-two people, again using a pre- and post-test design. The instrument is a revised questionnaire based on the National Training Laboratory model furnished by Dr. W. Warner Burke of the Institute for Applied Behavioral Science. The Self-descriptive Questionnaire, which is reproduced in Appendix C, has six main sections for self-evaluation: (1) communication, (2) group observation, (3) task skills, (4) responsiveness, (5) relation to group, and (6) self-awareness. A three-point rating scale is assigned for low, average, and high levels.

The Self-descriptive Questionnaire was given twice to the same group: once in January of 1968 and again ten weeks later. The sign test, indicating the significance of direction and degree of change, was found in Siegel.[10] The two sets of data were compared to determine if any significant changes in the student's self-assessment were found. If the numerical designation for a level of behavior was greater at the end of the workshop, a "plus" was assigned; and if less, a "minus."

Applying the sign test, a significant positive movement and direction of change were found. Seventeen people had positive differences greater than their negative ones. Two subjects had greater negative differences. Rejecting the null hypothesis, we concluded that a majority of the participants increased in their self-estimation; in their interpersonal and group skills. The sign test, however, did not measure change qualitatively but merely indicated the degree and direction of movement. Not all positive changes were desirable, such as "acting dominant toward others"; while a negative change in "making snap judgments" or "criticizing myself" would be considered more desirable. In the majority of scales, positive changes were indicative of improvement in interactive behavior. Again, it would be difficult to ascertain if behavior or attitude had observably changed or whether there was a lesser tendency to render "socially desirable" responses after the self-dis-

---

[10]Siegel, S.: *Non-Parametric Statistics for the Behavioral Sciences.* New York, McGraw, 1956.

closures of the workshop experience. Either change can be considered a positive gain.

This instrument has the advantages of rapid administration and ease of statistical analysis; also, it is of immediate relevance to the communication workshop objectives. Its continued use appears justified as a measure of student progress and course effectiveness and for further validation of the questionnaire itself as a research measure.

Videotape and Behavior Modification

Although our videotape research was limited, the potential serviceability of videotape use in facilitating change in behavior and in the self-concept warrants some discussion. Changes in self-concept might very well be a function of behavioral change. Videotape was seen as a potentially useful tool for acquainting the individual with his behaving self as it acts and reacts in the ongoing group experience. In such an encounter, it seemed profitable to offer the individual both objective feedback (coming from sources external to the group) and the opportunity to observe his group self and to respond to those behaviors, attitudes, and patterns of participation. In this way, the individual is encouraged to become more objective about his own behavior, which can be hypothesized as facilitating behavioral change.

Recent psychological research in the field of self-concept indicates that some relationship exists between "real-self, ideal-self correlations" and social adjustment. The reliability of the ideal self-concept, however, has been challenged by the research of Frank and Hiester.[11] The work of Bills, using the Index of Adjustment and Values, finds self-acceptance—regardless of ideal-self, real-self correlations—to be a more adequate measure of adjustment.[12] The findings of Stock and others, suggesting that acceptance of self can be correlated with acceptance of others, adds to the existing indications that self-acceptance is closely related to adjustment.[13]

---

[11]Frank, George H., and Hiester, Douglas S.: Reliability of the ideal-self concept. *J Counsel Psychol, XIV* (No. 4):356-357, 1967.

[12]Bills, R. E.; Vance, E. L., and McLean, O. S.: An index of adjustment and values. *J Consult Psychol, XV*:257-261, 1951.

[13]Stock, D.: An investigation into the interrelation between the self-concept and feelings directed toward other persons and groups. *J Consult Psychol, XIII*:176-180, 1949.

Jones' research, based upon his self-knowledge workshop design, indicates that a student-centered workshop in psychology and interpersonal relationships can potentially result in a significant increase in "self-acceptance," and by implication can lead to better adjustment.[14] Stoller later concurs with these findings when he says of freely interacting workshop groups:

> Such groups are particularly valuable in that they encourage people to interact in the context of providing a mirror for the effect a person has on others, a picture of how he moves through the world and when he tends to elicit from those he rubs up against . . . determining the discrepancy between that which he wishes to receive from the world and that which he makes the world give him; the difference between the interpersonal message he would like to give and the one he actually gives.[15]

Stoller further points out, however, that "One of the major technical problems in the field concerns the difficulties of presenting such feedback so as to facilitate its acceptance by the individual as well as maximizing its potential usefulness to him."[16] Kagan and his associates, in their studies on Interpersonal-Process-Recall, concluded that if a subject could be fed "enough cues to help him relive the experience, we could explore in depth at a later time various points in the interaction, the thoughts, feelings, changes in thoughts and feelings, and the meaning of various gestures and expressions."[17,18] Feedback that is offered in a print medium is obviously devoid of much of the intuitive feeling tone of the original interaction and lacks the cues necessary for a meaningful confrontation experience. Studies using still photography and audio recordings as feedback mechanisms have been conducted with some success by Cate,[19] Anderson,[20] and others. Nielsen was quite successful in

---

[14]Jones, Richard M.: The role of self knowledge in the education process. *Harvard Educ Rev, XXXII* (No. 2):200-209, spring 1962.

[15]Stoller, Frederick H.: The use of focused feedback via videotape in small groups. *Explorations in Human Relations Training*. Washington, D.C., National Training Laboratories, National Education Association, 1966.

[16]*Ibid.*

[17]Kagan, Norman; Krathwohl, David R., and Farquhar, William W.: Interpersonal process recall: Stimulated recall by videotape. In *Exploratory Studies of Counseling and Teaching-Learning*. East Lansing, Mich. State, 1965.

[18]Kagan, Norman; Krathwohl, David R., and Miller, Ralph: Stimulated recall in therapy using videotape—A case study. *J Counsel Psychol, X* (No. 3), 1964.

[19]Cate, C. A.; Cunningham, M. A., and Landsman, T.: To see oneself. *Educational Screen and Audiovisual Guide,* September, 1963, pp. 504-505.

[20]Anderson, Robert P., and Brown, Oliver H.: Tape recordings and counselor trainee understanding. *J Counsel Psychol, II* (No. 3): 189-194, 1955.

using the medium of sound film as a feedback device to facilitate self-confrontation.[21]

Recent advances in the field of closed-circuit television and videotape have opened new avenues of feedback use. Their availability on a wide scale has provided educational, psychological, and research concerns with a viable and practical feedback mechanism. As Stoller indicates:

> Videotape provides a new tool for enhancing the presentation of feedback. It has a number of advantages in that it involves the audiovisual channels of information; playback can be either immediate or delayed, selectivity is readily accomplished, repetition of viewing as well as stopping the action is very easy, and the tapes can be stored for as long as is required or can be used over again. Closed-circuit television cameras function quietly, modern equipment needs only ordinary room lighting for an excellent picture, and small cameras can be placed unobtrusively in a group setting.[22]

Furthermore, it seems apparent from most of the research and our own experience that conducting an encounter group in front of television cameras does not forfeit the spontaneity and naturalness of group interaction.

Videotape feedback also has the advantage of adding the recollected sensations of personal feeling, motives, and thoughts to the observable group situation. The group member observing himself on videotape is stimulated to evaluate his behavior in terms of what was happening *internally* during his interaction; he is thus required to scrutinize the source material of his observable pattern of participation—his own thoughts, feelings, and motives. Manifest behavior and subjective experiences are thereby synchronized into a meaningful whole, which gives the student a more complete picture of the why and how of his behavior in the group.

Much of the initial work done with videotape as a feedback device has been addressed to the problems of teacher-training. Other uses of videotape feedback have been made in counseling and counselor-training. The general finding of studies in this area is that the "mirror" function of videotape can impose upon the trainee an awareness of physical communication response patterns, effectiveness of stimuli, and a new, objective self-concept.

---

[21]Nielsen, Gerhard: *Studies in Self-Confrontation.* Cleveland, Howard Allen, 1964.

[22]Stoller, F. H.: The use of focused feedback via videotape in small groups. *Explorations in Human Relations Training.* Washington, D.C., National Training Laboratories, National Educational Association, 1966.

In addition to the use of videotape as a teaching-learning device and as a measure of progress and change, it can also be employed as a research instrument itself. Zajonc, at the University of Michigan, suggests a "cognitive tuning" technique that has application to persons viewing videotaped incidents and drawing conclusions stimulated by their observations. His research concludes that persons with more experience and knowledge in a particular area will be able to see more things (quantity) and more incisive kinds of things (quality) and will be able to organize those ideas into higher levels of abstraction than a control group. By using videotape of selected group encounters before experimental and control groups, we can hypothesize that, at the end of a workshop, the experimental group will be able to note and conceptualize more different kinds of behaviors and activities than a control group. This type of research waits upon the accumulation and validation of "selected group encounters" on videotape which is in process.

The final measure employed in our research and evaluation procedures was the subjective student evaluation, which permitted freedom for individual comment by its open-ended design. These evaluations are not readily reduced to statistically verifiable data but serve to give the reader an overview of the impact of the communication workshop on the participants as they saw, felt, and responded to it. A representative sampling has been appended to the sections on speaking skills, group process skills, and interpersonal communication.

Summary of Research Findings

Our research measures and findings have been limited in their applicability and usefulness. This is partly the fault of our practice and partly due to lack of valid and reliable testing instruments. Apparently, it is more difficult to measure "communication" than to measure the constructs of self-concept, interactive behavior, or other aspects of personality. Self-expression, poise, and openness can be observed more readily than evaluated by measuring instruments. In our program, both observations and self-evaluations were used, and some tentative generalizations may be made.

Our audiotape and videotape recordings provided some evidence of an increase in self-expression, openness, ease of participation, and interactive communication.

The pencil and paper inventories that were based on self-perceptions gave further evidence of the effect of the workshop on behavior and attitude, as students judged them. We saw some evidence on the FIRO-B of changes in expressed needs for affection and control by others; the Edwards schedule indicated "affiliation" needs for males and greater "autonomy" needs for females, suggesting mutual growth toward more congruence; the Leary checklist hinted at greater self-acceptance by the merging of ideal and real self-images; the Q-sort found the students becoming more articulate; and the Questionnaire indicated positive changes in the acquisition of group skills, more sensitive communication, and greater self-awareness. Finally, the student evaluations reveal a positive, if highly subjective, impact of the workshop on skill acquisition and on interpersonal sensitivity and communication. More credence than usual can be placed upon these responses, given the Antioch student's reputation for painful honesty and authenticity.

Generally, the workshop in communication achieved its purposes, as the various measures suggest, but whether most effectively in terms of time and effort remains yet to be tested by additional research with more rigorous methodology.

Part IV

CONCLUSIONS ABOUT THE PROGRAM

THIS MANUAL INDICATES something of the nature, development, and content of our program and illustrates one interdisciplinary approach to the communication process. If, as we believe, the traditional approach to speech-learning has definite limitations, then skills, techniques, and practice have a useful place; but they are not all that speech students require if they are to become effective communicators. Traditional speech courses do not necessarily enhance interpersonal and intrapersonal communication. A mix of methods and approaches is required, although they may not be included in one package. The student evaluations reinforce our decision to include the psychological, emotional, and sociological components of the total communicative process. Perhaps a more ideal structure would encompass a series of courses, workshops, and seminars over a longer period of time, each of which would cover some significant component of the whole: speaking skills, semantics, small-group process, mass media, communication theory, and interpersonal-relations training.

Our research measures and results admittedly have been inconclusive and inadequate. In part, this is the fault of our practice and in part the lack of valid and reliable testing instruments. Often, in the academic setting, a course is deemed successful when a "test" prepared by the instructor is "passed" by the student. Our intent was to look for both more objective and more subjective measures of change and learning. Excluding our video records, we were only partly successful in obtaining objective criteria. The Self-descriptive Questionnaire may prove to be the instrument of choice because it indicates changes in self-perception or self-concept after an interpersonal-communication experience, and the data can be handled statistically. Objective evidence, however, may be only a secondary consideration in evaluating courses of this kind, which are phenomenological in their impact. Tests that are content-centered or

63

measure deeply rooted personality factors appear to be equally inappropriate.

A group-centered approach to the teaching-learning process is highly demanding of all persons involved in it, and in its initial steps it can be beset with difficulties in the academic arena for both instructor and student. This is particularly so when, in the beginning, students themselves are suspicious, administrators skeptical, colleagues threatened or mistrustful, and even the instructor doubtful and uncertain. Nevertheless, this approach has pointed to the value of shared responsibility for learning that might serve, to some degree, the student demand for relevance and participation in the educational process. The interactive experience is not adjunctive but is essential to meaningful learning about groups and group processes. The exploration of a wider range of cognitive and theoretical material should most reasonably follow the experiential encounter, so that learning about small-group functioning should begin with participation in the small-group setting.

> If we as educators are to face the problem of meaninglessness, we must make an effort to conduct education in depth—to move toward something that is personally significant beyond the facade of facts, subject matter, logic, and reason behind which human motives and a person's real struggles and strivings are often concealed. This does not mean the rejection of subject matter—far from it—but it does mean helping the learner to relate himself to what he is learning and to fit what he learns into the fabric of his life in a meaningful way.[23]

From our experience, there appears to be good reason to recommend that sensitivity training be incorporated—and thereby legitimized—into undergraduate and graduate curricula. Called by any other name, it would still serve the ends of self-understanding and of awareness of feelings in self and others, and would free participants from the many barriers to growth, learning, and interpersonal communication. In our view, the T-group, or the encounter group, is a highly educational process and learning approach. Increasing use is being made of this approach in innovative adult programs around the country and at colleges and universities. Sensitivity training is found increasingly as an adjunct of psychology, sociology, education, management, human relations, and orientation

---

[23]Jersild, A. T.: *When Teachers Face Themselves.* New York, Teachers College, Columbia, 1955, p. 80.

courses. It is less frequently found in departments of speech or communication, which is unfortunate. It does require a supportive administration, a trained instructor who has himself been a participant in laboratory experiences, and a college or university climate conducive to innovation and experimentation. For instance, the University of Kansas at Lawrence has recently incorporated the Human Relations Center courses and activities into the Speech and Communication area. The General Motors Institute at Flint, Michigan, has reported an undergraduate course in Interpersonal Communication Theory. Interpersonal and intrapersonal communication is being given increasing attention in the speech offerings at Western Michigan University and at the new College of Interpersonal Communication at Ohio University. At Lesley College, sensitivity training and the "instrumental use of laboratory methods" is part of the required curriculum in its professional education program.

We can, without reservation, recommend the adoption of videotape recordings as a teaching-learning tool in settings where the focus is on the student and on his growth and interaction, rather than on the instructor. The speech portion of the communication workshop could be expanded to include more intensive videotaping of student practice and presentations. More use could be made of the videotape as a research instrument in the areas of feedback, confrontation, self-appraisal, kinesics, and the like; developing questionnaires, testing devices, and observation schedules appropriate to each area. Extensive research could be conducted in the area of social perception by drawing on critical incidents taken from workshop groups. Such a library could be used in both orientation and training programs and as a supplementary source of materials for the workshop itself.

The staff of our communications project again acknowledges its debt to those associates responsible for making this innovative program possible and highly rewarding for all who participated. Our debt has grown from our original creditors—the Jack Wolfram Foundation, and the Office of Program Development and Research in Education here at Antioch—to include a whole generation of college students who left their imprints on our work, on our tapes, and on our feelings about them and about ourselves.

Part V

ANNOTATED BIBLIOGRAPHY — BOOKS, FILMS, AND TAPES USED IN THE WORKSHOP

Books

Adult Educatoin Association: *The Leader's Digest.* Adult Education Association of the United States, 1953.

The *Digest* is a collection of reprints from *Adult Leadership Magazine,* interpreting the findings of social scientists in such a way as to make them of practical value to people in the field. The emphasis in this introductory work is on goals and functioning of small groups, member effectiveness, group effectiveness, program planning, use of resources, and basic group process.

Anderson, V. A.: *Training the Speaking Voice.* New York, Oxford U.P., 1961.

A basic text to be used as a course text in study of the science and art of the speaking process. Anderson presents a clear and simplified background of the physical-anatomical, physiological science of speech; he relates this theoretical background to a practical program of voice improvement.

Association for Supervision and Curriculum Development: *Perceiving, Behaving, Becoming; a New Focus for Education.* Association for Supervision and Curriculum Development, National Education Association, 1201 Sixteenth St., N.W., Washington, D.C. (A. W. Combs, Chairman).

A psychological approach to curriculum development oriented toward the development of the fully functioning and self-actualizing individual. This book draws on papers by Rogers, Maslow, and others of the self-actualizing, phenomenological school of psychology to develop the notion of a climate for self-actualization or "becoming."

Barbara, D. A. (Ed.): *Psychological and Psychiatric Aspects of Speech and Hearing.* Springfield, Thomas, 1960.

A collection of papers on speech, hearing, and communication from the point of view of the total personality. The studies contained here explore speech and hearing in terms of thought, personality, social structure, and the dynamics of interpersonal relationships. Included are sections on normal speech and hearing (and its psychological determinants), the psychopathology of speech and hearing disorders, psychotherapy of speech and hearing disorders, and the psychological implications of speech and hearing.

Bennis, Warren G.; Benne, Kenneth D., and Chin, Robert: *The Planning of Change.* New York, Holt, 1961.

One of the basic works on behavioral change, this collection of writings brings together some of the best conceptualizations and applications of the change process; it places these works in perspective with extensive critical and theoretical introductory material. Some emphasis is given to applied group dynamics and relevant material from several other social disciplines. Most of the material in this volume has been published since 1950.

Bennis, Warren; Schein, Edgar; Berlew, David, and Steele, Fred: *Interpersonal Dynamics: Essays and Readings on Human Interaction.* Homewood, Dorsey, 1964.

A collection of papers, the purpose of which is to "sketch out the conceptual territory and boundaries of the field of interpersonal relations more clearly than has been done before." The theoretical orientation of this work draws on symbolic interactionism (Durkheim, Cooley, Mead), on the interpersonal theory of social communication of Harry Stack Sullivan, object-relation and ego-theory psychology (neo-Freudians—Fairbairn, Klein, Bion), and existential psychology (Rogers, Maslow, May *et al.*). The editors include an orienting essay to introduce each section and fit it into their theoretical framework.

Berne, Eric: *Games People Play, The Psychology of Human Relationships.* New York, Grove, 1964.

Beginning with a brief expository section on the theoretical framework of transactional analysis, as set forth in his earlier work, Berne presents a casebook of material on game theory to the lay public. The material of the games is drawn from the observation of patterns in individual and group interactions which are substitutes for real intimacy and are characterized as "poignant forms of play." The focus here is on the recognition of such patterns of game behavior.

Bradford, Leland: *Human Forces in Teaching and Learning.* NTL (Selected

Reading Series No. 3.) Washington, D.C., National Education Association, 1961.

A collection of papers dealing with the little-acknowledged forces of social and emotional climate as they relate to the teaching and/or learning experience. The papers here, which develop the notion of social and emotional learning, are by Bradford, Benne, Lippitt, Gibb, Miles, and others.

Bradford, Leland P.; Gibb, Jack R., and Benne, Kenneth D.: *T-Group Theory and Laboratory Method.* New York, Wiley, 1964.

A collection of papers on the dynamics of behavioral, personal, and social change in the setting of the training group. The articles report some of the experimentation done in connection with the National Training Laboratories Institute, all dealing with the re-education of social relationships and human behavior. The book develops the idea of a "laboratory" method of learning, in which participants "are helped to diagnose and experiment with their own behavior and relationships in a specially designed environment"; the idea of experimenters and subjects collaborating in a learning experiment; the notion of a trainer, observers, laboratory communities, etc.; and the context for this type of educational experience.

Carpenter, Edmund, and McLuhan, Marshall: *Explorations in Communications.* Boston, Beacon, 1960.

An anthology of writings and essays taken primarily from *Explorations,* a journal in the field published at the University of Toronto, and including some pre-*Understanding Media* writing by Marshall McLuhan. Also included here are papers by Northrop Frye, David Reisman, and Gilbert Seldes. The premise of *Explorations* is, of course, that media—in particular, Western literacy, the printed word, and the electronic revolution—shape our consciousness more than we can or would like to recognize.

Cartwright, Dorwin, and Zander, Alvin (Eds.): *Group Dynamics: Research and Theory,* 2nd ed. Evanston, Row, Peterson, and Co., 1960.

A collection of readings which places the field of group dynamics in historical and theoretical perspective. Papers deal with determinants and consequences of group cohesiveness, with the nature of group pressures and the operation of group standards, with individual motives and the formation of group goals, and with interrelated topics of leadership and group performance, communication, power and status, and interpersonal relations. Of particular note are the introductory papers prepared by the editors, which serve to in‑ tegrate the ideas presented in each of six areas covered, as well as to point up the problems of research and theory in each section.

Cherry, Colin: *On Human Communication.* New York, Wiley, 1957.

A simplified approach to the area of communications drawn from the lectures of the author. The work, which Cherry says is not for "the experts," consists of a series of introductory essays on com‑ munication science, language, linguistics, semantics, syntactics, pragmatics, and the shape of the communicative process in general.

Collins, Barry E., and Guetzknow, Harold: *A Social Psychology of Group Processes for Decision Making.* New York, Wiley, 1964.

The authors develop a social psychology of group decision-mak‑ ing processes that is based upon empirical data in the field. This work concerns itself mainly with an inductive theory of encounter groups and does no more than imply applications in the field.

Eisenson, Jon; Auer, J. Jeffery, and Irwin, John V.: *The Psychology of Communication.* New York, Appleton, 1963.

A concise, compact text discussing the nature, origin, and pur‑ poses of speech; the neurological and psychological mechanisms that support and control it; and the communicative process among animals and among humans. Application of this information to individual and group communication includes the development of language in the child; the psychology of group discussion and of public communications systems; and the relationship between language and personality. A great deal of information is condensed into this comparatively short book. It is valuable, however, not only for the factual information it presents but also for the variety of experimental evidence it surveys, and the extensive bibliogra‑ phies at the end of each chapter.

Golembiewski, Robert T.: *The Small Group: An Analysis of Research Con‑ cepts and Operations.* Chicago, U. of Chicago, 1962.

This book ambitiously presents a broad foundation in the area of small-group research that is adequate both for the specialist and the student. Research analysis is the focus, as Golembiewski pre‑ sents the bulk of what has been learned in small-group analysis, thereby commenting upon the state and validity of present research in this area and also posing the questions and directions which will require further research. Of particular interest are the author's notes.

Gordon, Norton, J., and Wong, Helene H.: *A Manual for Speech Improvement.* Englewood Cliffs, Prentice-Hall, 1961.

The authors have developed a practical approach to basic speech develoment in the form of a manual based on general American speech and utilizing the International Phonetic Alphabet. The focus is on the language problems of Hawaiian and Southeast Asian students. This work is extremely useful in remedial work with students of bilingual background.

Gordon, Thomas: *Group-Centered Leadership: A Way of Releasing the Creative Power of Groups.* Cambridge, Houghton, 1955.

The author first develops a philosophy of constructive, democratic, participatory, creative groups, and then, in the genre of a case study, presents descriptive material based upon the application of this philosophy in the form of the effects of such group experience and the reactions of individuals who have experienced this type of group, their attitude and behavior changes, etc. In a third portion, the author describes and evaluates the application of this technique/theory/philosophy in an industrial organization.

Gray, Giles, W., and Wise, Claude M.: *The Bases of Speech.* New York, Harper, 1959.

This edition is an updated third revision of the original beginning text on *The Bases of Speech,* which gives more attention to the complex social bases of speech and adds to the material concerning the physical, acoustic basis of speech. The authors develop an expository book on the nature and function of speech for an advanced undergraduate level of study.

Hall, Edward Twitchell: *The Silent Language.* Garden City, Doubleday, 1959.

The author develops a context for, and deals with, nonverbal communication and awareness of meanings not expressed verbally. The emphasis here is on cross-cultural understanding of cues, gestures, posture, etc. This volume stands with the Reusch and Kees volume, *Nonverbal Communication,* as one of the basic works in that area.

Hare, Paul A.; Borgatta, Edgar F., and Bales, Robert F. (Eds.): *Small Groups: Studies in Social Interaction.* New York, Knopf, 1962.

A cross-disciplinary collection of papers from Lewin, Bales,

Cattell, Festinger, Newcomb, Tagiuri, Borgatta, Hare, Slater, and others, which deals with the basics of social interaction in the small group. Represented here are papers dealing with the historical development of small-group theory and research, with contemporary studies of social interaction in a group context, with the individual within the group, and with the group itself as a system of social interaction. A final section presents a comprehensive annotated bibliography of work in this field.

Hayakawa, S. I.: *Language in Thought and Action.* New York, Harcourt, 1949.

Begun as a revision of *Language in Action,* this work updates Hayakawa's earlier work and aims at acquainting the reader with the field of semantics. In a group setting, the focus of this study is relevant in terms of its attempt to get at human interaction through the mechanisms of linguistic communication.

Hoffmann, Randall W., and Plutchik, Robert: *Small Group Discussion in Orientation and Teaching.* New York, Putnam, 1959.

This work develops a foundation for use of the group-centered method in college orientation programs. The authors present much of the actual case material of ongoing orientation programs as well as a fairly extensive review of methodology, general principles, and philosophy of the group-centered method.

Jersild, Arthur T.: *In Search of Self.* New York, Bureau of Publications, Teachers College, Columbia, 1952.

Jersild presents the case for the encouragement of self-understanding in the child, presents empirical data and analyzes them, and develops from this material hypotheses which link self-understanding to understanding of others. This work stands as one of the basic papers advocating adoption by the educational institution of the principles of self-psychology.

Kemp, C. Gratton: *Perspectives on the Group Process; A Foundation for Counseling with Groups.* Boston, Houghton, 1964.

Drawing upon the disciplines of psychology, sociology, education, and religion, the editor presents a collection of papers about the potentials for change, in the group context, for the individual and for the group. Designed for audiences involved in various aspects of higher education, this work explores both the interdisciplinary foundations of group theory and the nature of the ongoing group process.

Klein, Alan F.: *Role Playing in Leadership Training and Group Problem Solving.* New York, Assn. Pr., 1956.

Klein develops the technique of role-playing by taking the reader through the process from beginning to end, providing detailed instructions at every step along the way. Much illustrative material is included. This is a rather basic how-to-do-it book that explores the selection, planning, design, function and use of role-playing.

Knowles, Malcolm and Hulda: *Introduction to Group Dynamics.* New York, Assn. Pr., 1959.

A short introduction to group dynamics. The authors briefly explain some background of group-dynamics work, some theoretical foundations of group-dynamics research, and some applications. Included is a list of readings for follow-up.

Lee, Irving J.: *How to Talk with People.* New York, Harper, 1952.

Starting with the premise that most interpersonal communication is talking *to* people rather than *with* people, Lee presents the case for understanding and rapport in interpersonal relationships. His summary of findings and suggestions is a useful guide to the kinds of communication problems frequently encountered in a group setting.

Lewin, Kurt: *Resolving Social Conflicts; Selected Papers on Group Dynamics.* New York, Harper, 1948.

A collection of papers, monographs, and articles by Lewin designed and presented as a convenient sourcebook in Lewinian social psychology and a logical progression of Lewinian thought.

Lifton, Walter M.: *Working with Groups: Group Process and Individual Growth.* New York, Wiley, 1961.

The author presents a theoretical framework for behavior change that is strongly grounded in the phenomenological and client-centered approach. Beginning with the individual's perception of a situation, Lifton works through helping behavior and change in terms of approaching problems of immediate concern in a secure and trusting group setting, and develops this theoretical position to a point where changes in the individual's behavior become generalized and involve changes in other areas. Lifton describes personality as an ever-changing thing and the group as the context for productive change.

Lippitt, Gordon (Ed.): *Leadership in Action.* (Pamphlet, NTL Selected

Reading Series No. 2.) National Education Association, 1201 Sixteenth Street, N.W., Washington, D.C., 1961.

A collection of the outstanding articles in the field of leadership and leadership training, collected from 1945-1961. This collection contains writings by Lippitt, Benne, Deutsch, Bradford, Tannenbaum, and others, and provides a sound basis for introductory leadership theory and group dynamics.

Malamud, Daniel I., and Machover, Solomon: *Toward Self-Understanding, Group Techniques in Self-Confrontation.* Springfield, Thomas, 1965.

This book explores the content, process, structure, and results of the encounter workshop, or the Workshop in Self-Understanding. The model here is a series of structured classroom experiences centering on confrontation as the chief vehicle of the course. The reader is presented with a bulk of material concerning the background, application, validity, and results of such a vehicle, and then is presented with an extensive section on leading such a workshop group. The latter section contains much valuable material on the content, process, and exercises possible in this kind of confrontation workshop.

Maslow, Abraham H.: *Toward a Psychology of Being.* Princeton, Van Nostrand, 1962.

One of the basic works dealing with the concepts involved in a psychology of self-actualization. Maslow develops the links between motivation and growth and between cognition and growth, leading finally to the primary formulations of an existential psychology. A bibliography is included.

May, Rollo: *Man's Search for Himself.* New York, Norton, 1953.

This work on self-actualization directs itself to the issues of a wide reading public, drawing upon life experiences and existential psychology. May deals quite adequately with the major flow of ideas present in a self-actualizing psychology, loneliness, anxiety, freedom, creativity, and "becoming". Rather than presenting the material as a text in the area, however, May has preferred to present his material in a way which catalyzes introspection and reflection.

Mayer, Lyle V.: *Notebook for Voice and Diction.* Dubuque, Brown, W.C., 1960.

In addition to presenting a notebook, the author has attempted to link theory and study to practice and application. The book contains theoretical discussions, drills, exercises, and practice selections, and is designed to be used in full-class or individual self-help programs for speech improvement.

McLuhan, H. Marshall: *Understanding Media,* New York, McGraw, 1964.

Drawing upon his wide literary background and his previous writings in the field of communications, McLuhan presents his phantasmagoria of "inconographiti," which serves to present a single overwhelming motif to the reader. McLuhan's message is that contemporary society pays too much attention to content and not enough to process, the result being a lack of awareness of the ways in which the environment shapes the consciousness and orientation of the individual and of the society. Although this work was intended to be primarily an explorative and reflective investigation of media and involvement, McLuhan's idea of all-at-onceness are directly relevant to the concerns of an encounter group dealing in the here-and-now.

Menninger, Karl: *Love Against Hate.* New York, Harcourt, 1942.

Menninger grapples with one of the basic issues of interpersonal behavior, favoring the life or love instinct over the hate or death instinct. Much of the psychological background for competitive behaviors is presented to cultivate the human capacity for warm, loving interpersonal relationships.

Miles, Matthew B.: *Learning to Work in Groups: A Program Guide for Educational Leaders.* New York, Bureau of Publications, Teachers College, Columbia, 1959. (Publication of the Horace Mann Lincoln Institute of School Experimentation.)

In a comprehensive source book, Miles concerns himself with the improvement of the quality of work in small face-to-face, primarily task-oriented, groups within public school settings. The focus is on the training process, from a discussion of the need, meaning, and uses of the training, through planning, designing, and the evaluation of the training activities and experience. Of particular interest are the chapters on the problems involved in assuming the trainer role, and the chapter which presents a wide range of specific training activities.

Missildine, W. Hugh: *Your Inner Child of the Past.* New York, S. and S., 1963.

Missildine rethinks the dynamics of interpersonal relationships around the notion that the child is inevitably present as an important influence in the dynamics of present adult relationships. If this "child within" can be understood in terms of the origin of attitudes and values, then such knowledge can be used in effectively dealing with others. Missildine discusses the most obvious of parental characteristics affecting the inner child of the past that have the most significant impact upon adult modes of behavior.

Nichols, Ralph G., and Stevens, Leonard A.: *Are You Listening?* New York, McGraw, 1957.

The authors begin with a defense of listening as one of man's prime sources of information input, and proceed to present their thesis that listening can be improved (to extend beyond our average of 25% listening efficiency) through instructional programs, training, and practice, in much the same way as with other communicative skills.

Nielsen, Gerhard: *Studies in Self-Confrontation; Viewing a Sound Motion Picture of Self and Another Person in a Stressful Dyadic Interaction.* Copenhagen, Munksgaard, and Cleveland, Howard Allen, 1964.

One of the basic works on the use of media as a feedback device in a setting of interpersonal interaction, Nielsen develops the idea and theoretical framework for the research upon which he reports. His orientation is the synchronization of recall (thoughts and feelings at the time a film of an interaction was made) with actual behaviors as evidenced by the film. Nielsen develops out of the framework of self-confrontation an integration of self-theory with nonverbal behavior (in terms of eye and body movements and idiosyncratic body movements) theory and develops a context for later research in memory, recall, and confrontation. The final chapter here points toward use of self-confrontation in a therapy setting.

Rogers, Carl: *On Becoming a Person.* Boston, Houghton, 1961.

This work represents a collection of papers drawn from Rogers' recent clinical experience and research. The work is aimed at the "intelligent layman" and lends depth and perspective to Rogers' theories of client-centered relationships. Rogers illustrates this work with excerpts taken from recorded therapy interviews. The book successfully deals with the constructs of phenomenological, existential, person-centered psychology.

Ruesch, Jurgen, and Kees, Weldon: *Nonverbal Communication; Notes on the Visual Perception of Human Relations*. Berkeley, U. of Calif., 1956.
In a largely pictorial investigation, the authors explore the little-known channels of human communication that do not require speech. The authors build a theoretical and conceptual framework for the whole system of nonverbal communication and interpretation. Photographs illustrate the diverse effects that action, objects, and words can produce. This work culminates in the development by the authors of a theory of nonverbal communication.

Schutz, William B.: *Joy*. New York, Grove, 1967.
A refreshing integration of theory and practice aimed at freeing the individual and rendering him a more joyous person. Dr. Schutz develops this work out of research and laboratory experience at Esalen Institute and at the National Training Laboratories. The releasing process, actually a diverse assortment of exercises and techniques, is approached physically through body movement, through personal functioning and interpersonal relationships, and through organizations. Generally, Schutz has captured the exciting applications of some of the more promising trends toward self-realization and self-actualization in contemporary education and psychology.

Shepherd, Clovis R.: *Small Groups: Some Sociological Perspectives*. San Francisco, Chandler Pub., 1964.
Starting with the definition of a small group as "two or more people interacting," Shepherd develops an inductive approach, making research reader-relevant. This work also includes useful abstracts and bibliographical materials.

Tannenbaum, Robert; Weschler, Irving R., and Massarik, Fred: *Leadership and Organization: A Behavioral Science Approach*. New York, McGraw, 1961.
A collection of writings of the members of a Human Relations Research Group (HRRG) and of the National Training Laboratories covering a period from 1950-1960, with comments, additions, and critiques from experts in the field added. This volume is intended as an overview and covers the areas of leadership and the influence process, sensitivity training, and organizational process.

Weschler, Irving R., and Reisel, Jerome: *Inside a Sensitivity Training Group*. Los Angeles, Institute of Industrial Relations, U. of Calif., 1960.
A short and easily read work presenting the background and

theory of sensitivity training as well as a great deal of insightful material drawn from the experience of the laboratory situation. It gives the chronological developments of a particular lab group in a frame of reference which broadens understanding of T-group theory.

Films

Twelve Angry Men. A film starring Henry Fonda, produced for the commercial market, which explores group dynamics through the decision-making process of a jury committed to the task of deciding a man's fate in a murder case. (BW, Feature length).

The Alphabet Conspiracy. A simplified overview of the speaking and communication process, covering the physiology, sociology, phonetic, and electronic aspects of human speech. (Bell Telephone, Color, 60 Min.)

Task of the Listener. A kinescope of S.I. Hayakawa, who discusses communication from the general semantic view, highlighting the importance of nonevaluative listening. The material is excellent, although the presentation is somewhat dated. (National Educational Television: KQED, 1956, BW, 30 minutes. One of the "Language in Action" series available from Film Library, Indiana University, Bloomington, Indiana, 47401).

More Than Words. Although this film is oriented toward industry, the producer deals less with technique and more in terms of our feelings about communication and how one goes about it. The guide book accompanying the film goes in another direction; although attractively presented, it is somewhat simplistically written to communicate something other than the film. This film might possibly provide introductory material. (Color, 14 minutes. Available as part of series on "Communication" by producer Henry Strauss & Co., 31 W. 53rd Street, New York City, 10019.)

A Communications Primer. A modern, neatly animated, though somewhat tedious elucidation of the basic model of communication. The message is followed from the source of information (or selection), and coding (or transmission), across the communications channel to its decoding (by the receptor), at the ultimate destination. A couple of elementary principles of information theory (exponential increase of information per bit; noise/redundancy) are also presented. An attempt is made to drive home the point that no message can be communicated unless the receptor is compatible with the transmitter. (Color, 22 minutes. Available free through Herman Miller Furniture Company, Zeeland, Michigan).

The Speech Chain. This animated film traces the speaking process from its inception in the speaker's brain to its reception by the listener.

Physical and biological links in the process are diagramed and animated. (Color, 19 minutes, Bell Telephone).

The Dynamics of Leadership. This series of films includes "Anatomy of a Group," "Roadblock to Communication," and others under the editorship of Dr. Malcolm Knowles. The catalog, "Films in the Behavioral Sciences," is available on loan from the Pennsylvania State University, Psychological Cinema Register, University Station, Pennsylvania.

Communication Theory and the New Educational Media. This film series is annotated in the Ohio State University brochure available from the Department of Photography, Motion Picture Division, Ohio State University, 1885 Neil Avenue, Columbus, Ohio 43210.

The "Berlo" Communication Series. These series are aimed at business and industry and are available either through the University of Minnesota at Minneapolis, or through the Bureau of National Affairs, 1231 24th Street N.W., Washington, D.C. 20037.

The Speak Up Series. A series of half-hour kinescopes from the University of Michigan Television Library, cover the organization of formal speaking situations, committee meetings, program planning, and other speaking and listening skills and techniques. The host is Professor N. E. Miller of the Speech Department with guests from other university speech departments. The listing is available from the University of Michigan, 310 Maynard Street, Ann Arbor, Michigan.

Other film sources are the larger university film libraries, such as at Indiana University and the University of California at Berkeley.

Tapes

An Anthology of Human Communication. Patterns of interaction in actual therapy sessions plus basic concepts of communication. (Paul Watzlawick, Palo Alto, California, Science and Behavior Books, Inc., 1964.)

Case of Jim. Excerpts and discussion of psychotherapeutic sessions with a college stutterer having concomitant personality problems—a Rogerian, client-centered approach. (Julius Seeman, Nashville, Tennessee, American Guidance Service, 1957.)

Conference Leadership. A discussion of the role of the group leader in creating an atmosphere conducive to creative participation. (Nathaniel Cantor, Cincinnati, Sound Seminars.)

Effective Listening. A two-hour program (learning frames with accompanying manual) to improve individual listening skill. (New York, Basic Systems, Inc., 1964.)

Language: Key to Human Understanding. Dr. Hayakawa discusses the importance of nonevaluative listening in the process of communication. (Cincinnati, Sound Seminars. Presented before the American Humanist Society.)

Language and Man. A series of five tapes which give the historical and linguistic background of modern languages and the factors in language change.

Science of Sound. A brief review of the physical nature of sound: intensity frequency, and quality. (Bell Telephone Laboratories, 1958.)

Ways of Mankind—A Word in Your Ear. A study in language as affected by time, place, sex, and culture. (Lester Sinclair *et al.* Produced by the National Association of Educational Broadcasters under the supervision of Professor Walter Goldschmidt.)

Where Minds Meet. A series of tapes from Western Michigan University on various aspects of communicative relationships and interactions. (Freund, Nelson Series.)

Human Development Institute (HDI). A series of five program booklets for two students to study together to improve communication skills. (Human Development Institute, Inc., 1299 W. Peachtree Street, N.E., Atlanta, Georgia, 1965.)

Part VI

Appendix A

SYLLABUS FOR
COMMUNICATION SKILLS AND
INTERPERSONAL RELATIONS

This composite course is an outgrowth of several years of experimental efforts in the Antioch Communication Program, originally sponsored by the Jack Wolfram Foundation, which shares with us a continuing concern for achieving effective and meaningful communication.

Objectives

The course combines the theory and practice of basic communication experiences in speaking skills, small-group interaction, and human relations. It seeks the development of confidence in self-expression and increased personal effectiveness in all communicative settings.

Videotape and audiotape recordings are utilized as a teaching-learning aid in self-confrontation and in awareness of group processes. The interpersonal-communication component utilizes encounter groups (T-groups) to provide opportunity for openness, authenticity, and fuller awareness of self and others.

Procedures

The class will meet three times weekly for 2 hours each meeting:
Tuesday, Thursday, and *Saturday* 10 A.M. - 12 noon
The first eight class meetings on speaking skills will be highly structured and highly intensive. It will proceed in a traditional manner, using lectures, presentations, assignment of readings, and preparations for class. The next six meetings will utilize group-centered leadership within a workshop setting, while the remainder of the quarter will consist of unstructured encounter-group sessions.

Education Majors

A special syllabus found in the Bookstore will be used for practice teaching in Speech. An additional hour's meeting time for supervision and discussion for all education majors will need to be found.

Bibliography

Attached, you will find a list of books, pamphlets, program texts, and audiotapes. Tapes and record collections are in the second floor of the library; most books are on 1-day reserve in the stacks; 2-hour materials are in the reserve section and are marked here with an asterisk. The bibliography is divided into separate sections, reflecting the course components.

Evaluations

Grades will be determined by an individual conference between student and instructor. These will be based on both objective and subjective evidence: speech improvement, knowledge, and skill in group diagnosis-participation; the student's assessment of his own progress and growth.

Speaking and Listening Skills (Weeks 1-3)

I. The purpose of this part of the course is to help the student develop a more effective and pleasing speaking voice; to acquire some knowledge of the speaking process and its mechanism; and to provide practice in formal speech presentations.

   A. Exercises and practice to improve articulation, resonance, and expressiveness.

   B. Oral reading presentations from prose, poetry, and Shakespeare.

   C. Preparation and delivery of impromptu and formal speeches.

   Speech and Voice Practice

   During the first 3 weeks of the quarter, all students should plan to practice speech exercises from 1/2 hour to a full hour daily, much as you would do with a new musical instrument. A scheduled time in music practice rooms or empty classrooms (not social or living space) is recommended. After the third week, only selected students will be asked to continue this practice routine.

   Recordings

   Changes in speaking skills will be measured by audiotape and videotape recordings. See attached "Recording Material" to be presented the first class meeting. A progress recording check will be made at the 8th meeting, and a final recording at the end of the quarter.

II. Class Calendar (1st through 3rd week; T. Th. S., 10-12)

   1st Meeting—Introduction to course
      1. Lecture on Elements of Speech.

2. Recordings: Audio and video.
3. *Assignment*: Read in one of the speech texts (Brown, Anderson, Hibbit . . .), fill out Questionnaire. Prepare 3-5 minute reading from prose: short story, fable, legend.

2nd Meeting

1. Exercises.
2. Lecture on Sound-production Mechanism.
3. Readings and critique.
4. Arrange playback time of first recording.
5. *Assignment*: Continue textual reading. Practice 1/2 to 1 hour daily. Listen to tape: *Speech as Creative Medium*.

3rd Meeting

1. Exercises.
2. Lecture-demonstration on Interpretation: phrasing, emphasis variety.
3. Prose readings (continued).
4. *Assignment*: Continue in speech books. Prepare readings on modern poetry. Listen to a poetry recording-audio-visual.

4th Meeting

1. Exercises.
2. Lecture on Sounds of English.
3. Readings of poetry.
4. *Assignment*: Listen to a Shakespearean play. Prepare a Shakespearean selection. Continue exercises and reading.

5th Meeting

1. Shakespearean readings.
2. Discussion of public speaking and outlining.
3. *Assignment*: Read Green, "Speak to Me," or/and "Outlining and Organization." Prepare 3-minute talk, plus outline.

6th Meeting

1. First speeches and outlines. Videotape.
2. Critique and playbacks.
3. *Assignment*: Prepare second speech and outline. Conclude readings in public-speaking books.

7th Meeting

1. Second speeches and outlines. Critiques.
2. Playbacks.
3. *Assignment*: Recording check for next meeting. Prepare

materials. Listen to tapes: *Effective Listening*. Begin readings
on group process.

8th Meeting

1. Recordings and playbacks; critique.
2. *Assignment*: Continue readings on group process.

Prepare for 1st Class Meeting

RECORDING MATERIAL

I. THIS IS   (name)   SPEAKING. TODAY IS   (date)   .
    YOU ARE NOW HEARING A SAMPLE OF MY SPEAKING VOICE. I WILL
    FIRST READ A PARAGRAPH ENTITLED "THE RAINBOW PASSAGE."
    *When the sunlight strikes raindrops in the air, they act like a
    prism and form a rainbow. The rainbow is a division of white light
    into many beautiful colors. These take the shape of a long round
    arch with its path high above and its two ends apparently beyond
    the horizon. When a man looks for something beyond his reach, his
    friends say that he is looking for the pot of gold at the end of the
    rainbow.*

II. NEXT I WILL READ FROM POETIC MATERIAL. Choose one of the fol-
    lowing two poems to read:

THE LESSON OF THE MOTH

I was talking to a moth the other evening
He was trying to break into an electric light bulb
        and fry himself on the wires
Why do you fellows pull this stunt, I asked him
Because it is the conventional thing for moths, or why?
If that had been an uncovered candle instead of an electric light bulb
You would now be a small unsightly cinder, have you no sense?
        *"Plenty of it" he answered, "but at times we get tired of
        using it."*
We get bored with the routine, and crave beauty and excitement.
        Fire is beautiful and we know that if we get too close,
It will kill us, but what does that matter?
It is better to be happy for a moment, and be burned up with beauty
than to live a long time and be bored all the while
        So we wad all our life up into one little roll
and then we shoot the roll. . . . That's what life is for!

It is better to be a part of beauty for one instant and then
cease to exist than to exist forever and never be a part of beauty
　　　Our attitude toward life is come easy, go easy!
We are like human beings used to be before they became
too civilized to enjoy themselves!

And before I could argue him out of his philosophy,
he went and immolated himself on a patent cigar lighter,
　　　I do not agree with him myself, I would rather have
half the happiness and twice the longevity. . . .
　　　But at the same time I wish there was something I wanted
as badly as he wanted to fry himself. . . .

　　　　　　　　　　　　　　　—Don Marquis

RICHARD III

Now is the winter of our discontent
Made glorious summer by this sun of York:
And all the clouds that lour'd upon our house
In the deep bosom of the ocean buried.
Now are our brows bound with victorious wreaths;
Our bruised arms hung up for monuments;
Our stern alarums changed to merry meetings,
Our dreadful marches to delightful measures.
Grim-visaged war hath smooth'd his wrinkled front;
And now, instead of mounting barbed steeds
To fright the souls of fearful adversaries,
He capers nimbly in a lady's chamber
To the lascivious pleasing of a lute.
But I, that am not shaped for sportive tricks,
Nor made to court an amorous looking-glass;
I, that am rudely stamp'd, and want love's majesty
To strut before a wanton ambling nymph;
I, that am curtail'd of this fair proportion,
Cheated of feature by dissembling nature,
Deform'd, unfinish'd, sent before my time
Into this breathing world, scarce half made up,
And that so lamely and unfashionable
That dogs bark at me as I halt by them;
Why, I, in this weak piping time of peace,
Have no delight to pass away the time,
Unless to spy my shadow in the sun,

And descant on mine own deformity:
And therefore, since I cannot prove a lover,
I am determined to prove a villain,
And hate the idle pleasures of these days.

—Shakespeare

III. FINALLY, I WILL TALK ABOUT AN INCIDENT FROM MY OWN EXPERI-
ENCE IN COMMUNICATION. (About 1-2 minutes—giving or getting
directions on a trip or co-op job; an experience with stage fright; an
unusual conversation with a stranger, foreigner, police officer, blind
date, mental patient, prospective employer, Arabian oil-well digger,
etc.)

VOICE-TRAINING ANALYSIS

Speaker: Class: Date:

RATE	*FORCE*	*PITCH*
too fast _____	adequate _____	high _____
too even _____	weak _____	low growl _____
poor phrasing _____	unvaried _____	monotone _____
faculty duration _____	pattern _____	narrow range _____
use of pause _____	loud _____	high overtones _____
staccato rhythm _____		good level _____

ARTICULATION	*QUALITY*	*MISCELLANEOUS*
oral inactivity _____	nasal _____	tight jaw _____
dull (s) _____	denasal _____	dialect _____
whistled (s) _____	breathy _____	posture _____
side of mouth _____	strained _____	fluency _____
overprecise _____	throaty _____	mispronunciations _____
substitutions _____	husky _____	facial expression _____
distortions _____	flat _____	nervousness _____
final consonants _____	lifeless _____	confidence _____
	resonant _____	
	variety and	
	expressiveness _____	

COMMENTS: _____

_____

Exercises to improve voice and speech should include:

_____ freeing the jaw	_____ variety of fast-slow,	_____ singing scales and
_____ slow rate	high-low, loud-soft	songs
_____ use of pause	_____ general emotional	_____ recite songs; sing
_____ prolonging vowels	expressiveness	readings
_____ exaggerated articu-	_____ reading aloud	_____ humming
lation	_____ projection	_____ lower pitch register
		_____ voice placement

SPEECH EXERCISES FOR DAILY PRACTICE

I. Relaxation and Medical Breathing
1. Relax muscles of face and jaw by shaking head gently from side to side, permitting jaw to move as if loosely connected.
2. Yawn and sigh; repeat saying "ya . . ya . . ya" with minimum effort.
3. Place a book against your abdomen; inhale and exhale at varying lengths of time, vary again by inhaling quickly and exhaling on (s), then (m), and (ah). Repeat with hands folded back at the wrist, on lower ribs. Note lateral movement with each breath.
4. Count as far as you can on one breath. Recite the alphabet slowly, once through, connecting all the sounds in a chanting tone and articulating each sound with exaggerated care.

II. Projection
1. Pant easily, then laugh on "ha . . ha . . ha . . ho . . ho . . ho" and observe the short pulses of air and the forceful contraction of the belt muscles. This is the source of energy.
2. Repeat rhythmically "hoo-ho-hah-hey," first at a whisper level, then half-tone and half-whisper, then at conversational loudness, and finally, without tightening or straining the throat, at full singing intensity.
3. *Sing* the following phrases forcefully but keep the throat as relaxed as possible.
   READY! AIM! FIRE!
   FORWARD MARCH!
   SHIP AHOY
   FOUR BELLS AND ALL'S WELL
   OPEN IN THE NAME OF THE LAW!
   CRY "GOD FOR HARRY, ENGLAND AND ST. GEORGE!"
4. Read the following forcefully, yet with contrast, from soft through loud to very loud. Read ideas or thought groups (phrases) rather than words. Pause for effect and for breath at the diagonal lines:
   Romans, countrymen, and lovers!/ hear me for my cause;/ and be silent, that you may hear./ /Believe me for mine honor;/ and have respect for mine honor, that you may believe./ /. . . Had you rather Caesar were living/ /and die all slaves,/ than that Caesar were dead,/ to live all free men?/ /As Caesar loved me, I weep for him;/ as he was

fortunate, I rejoice at it;/ /as he was valiant, I honor him/ but as he was ambitious,/ I slew him.

III. Pitch Variation and Oral Resonance

1. Sing (ah) five notes up and down the scale on one breath, increasing the force and prolonging the top note. Practice until the same 5-note scale can be repeated five times on one breath.

2. Starting at your lowest singing tone, sing a 5-note scale and after each descent, start a half-tone higher until you gradually reach your highest singing tone. Then descend, a half-step down each time.

3. First sing the following carol, then recite it. Retain as many of the singing values as you can as you recite: open jaw, vowel stress, pitch variation, slow tone duration, and projection.

    It came upon a midnight clear
    That glorious song of old,
    From angels bending near the earth,
    To touch their harps of gold.
    "Peace on the earth, good will to men,"
    From heaven's all gracious king,
    The world in solemn stillness lay,
    To hear the angels sing.

4. Practice scales and a variety of songs in the above manner, first singing, then reciting and maintaining singing qualities.

5. Choose a prose or a poetry selection such as the following, and first chant it on one tone emphasizing loudness, slow rate, and vowel stress. Repeat singing the selections using a wide melodic range; and finally, recite it, retaining some of the singing qualities.

    Four score and seven years ago our fathers brought forth on this continent, a new nation, conceived in Liberty, and dedicated to the proposition that all men are created equal.

    . . . It is rather for us to be here dedicated to the great task remaining before us—that from these honored dead we take increased devotion to that cause for which they gave the last full measure of devotion—that we here highly resolve that these dead shall not have died in vain—that this nation, under God, shall have a new birth of freedom— and that government of the people, by the people, for the people, shall not perish from the earth.

    Call me Ishmael. Some years ago—never mind how long pre-

cisely—having little or no money in my purse, and nothing
particular to interest me on shore, I thought I would sail
about a little and see the watery part of the world. It is
a way I have of driving off the spleen, and regulating the
circulation. Whenever I find myself growing grim about the
mouth; whenever it is a damp, drizzly November in my soul . . .
then, I account it high time to get to sea as soon as I can.

The curfew tolls the knell of parting day
The lowing herd winds slowly o'er the lea
The ploughman homeward plods his weary way,
And leaves the world to darkness and to me.
Now fades the glimmering landscape on the sight
And all the air a solemn stillness holds,
Save where the beetle wheels his droning flight.
And drowsy tinklings lull the distant folds.

IV. Nasal Resonance and Voice Consonant Stress

1. Begin humming by rapidly repeating "boom, boom, boomboom-boommmmm . . m-m-m-m-m-m-mmmmmmmm," until a tingling and vibrating sensation is felt on lips and nose.

2. Hum, then chant, stressing the nasal sounds (m,n,ng). Remember that the final (s) is pronounced as a (z) when following voiced sounds:

   The moon never beams without bringing me dreams . . . .
   Mumbo, Jumbo, God of the Congo . . .
   The moan of doves in immemorial elms, and the hum of
   *   innumerable bees.*

3. Repeat but, instead of chanting, speak the above sentences retaining the nasal stress.

4. Hum up and down the scales. Repeat using "mum."

5. Read the following, stressing all of the continuant voice consonants including the nasals (vvvv), (zzzz), (zh) (as in measure), (th) (as in then and brother).

   I am thy father's spirit; Doomed for a certain term to walk
   the night, and for the day confined toffast in fires, till
   the foul crimes done in my days of nature are burnt and
   purged away.

   So live, that when thy summons comes to join
   The innumerable caravan that moves
   To that mysterious realm, where each shall take
   His chamber in the silent halls of death.

Abide with me; fast falls the even-tide; the darkness deepens. Lord, with me abide.

V. Read Aloud From Poetry, or Poetic Prose

Stress nasals, pitch variation, phrasing and pause, vowel stress and melody within the phrase; projection, articulation, variety and expressiveness.

PUBLIC-SPEAKING OUTLINE ORGANIZATION

Purpose of Speech

1. *Exposition*: To inform, describe, demonstrate, lecture.
2. *Persuasion*: To change ideas or attitudes.
3. *Action*: To move audience, to initiate action.
4. *Entertainment*: To amuse or provide aesthetic experience.
5. *Other*: To eulogize, commemorate, introduce.

Prepare Speech

1. Determine purpose (as above) in respect to audience.
2. List possible topics.
3. Choose and write topic in form of central idea.
4. Subdivide topic into component parts.
5. Research facts and ideas.
6. Outline main ideas with supporting illustrative facts or examples.
7. Prepare introduction, conclusion, and outline.
8. Prepare speaking notes.
9. Practice.

Outline of Speech

I. *Introduction* (about 10% of total time)

    A. *Get attention*

        Striking statement, quotation, question, special interest of audience, significance of subject, humor, arouse curiosity, use of pause, honest compliment, familiar local reference, previous speaker said, reference to common ground between speaker and audience.

    B. *Orient the audience*

        State purpose or central idea, give background, or explain your interest in the subject.

    C. *Give the audience a reason for listening*

        Usefulness of topic value or benefit to audience, explain how subject touches some need or interest of audience.

II. Body of speech
  A. *Main points*
    1. Natural dimensions of central idea.
    2. Use two or three main points organized in sequential or logical pattern.
  B. *Organizational patterns*
    1. *Topical* (division depends on the topic): Skin-diving equipment provides for underwater breathing, vision, and action in comfort and safety.
    2. *Chronological*: Past, present, and future—or sequential steps in a process or action.
    3. *Spatial*: North, East, South, West; top to bottom, front to back, relation between points, geographically or spatially (circulation of traffic, blood, or internal-combustion engine).
    4. *Problem-solution*: Start with the problem and suggest one or more solutions (problem: teacher shortage due to low salary scale; solution: raise salaries through taxes).
    5. *Cause and effect* (or the reverse): a. People are careless about their camping fires. b. Resultant loss from forest fires.
    6. *Importance*: Arrange points in order of their importance or significance, beginning or ending with the most important point.
  C. *Supporting material*
    To make the main point clear, interesting, or logical, showing how needs or problems can be met by visualizing them.
    1. *Comparison or contrast*: Compare with something known and familiar (submarine is as long as a football field; badminton is like tennis; chess is like checkers).
    2. *Evidence or statement of authority:* Prove assertions with facts and examples.
  a. Examples:
    A specific instance—a small story with facts, names, dates, places.
  b. Testimony: Use quotation of authority known to audience.
    3. *Explanation*: Who, what, where, why, how, and when. Giving broad understanding or specific detailed working knowledge. Give audience knowledge first to capture their interest. Use statistics.
    4. *Description*: Create a mental image of your ideas and use vivid, colorful, and accurate language.

5. *Illustration*: A longer story; an extended example. Story tells about the speaker's idea in this form.
6. *Restatement*: Rephrase your purpose or subject sentence two or three times: "Let me put it another way. . . ." Also restate and rephrase each main point before going on to the next. Gives emphasis and aids clarity.
7. *Use visual aids*: Blackboard, graph, chart, picture, model, piece of equipment (large enough for audience to see easily). Do not talk to the board or equipment.

III. Conclusion of speech (about 5% of total time)
Draw the thoughts and ideas together effectively.
Summarize the main points.
Tell a brief story applying your points to some immediate problem.
Use a striking quotation: "Civilization is a race between education and catastrophe."
Make a final appeal for support, change, action, resolve, allegiance.
Give an emotionalized or idealized statement of the thesis.

Group Process (weeks 4-6)

Purpose

A. To provide some initial theory of, and practice in, small-group functioning.
B. To understand better how problems are solved and decisions are reached in group settings.
C. To develop specific skill and competence in:
    1. Diagnosing group difficulties.
    2. Observing group process objectively.
    3. Understanding and practicing leadership functions.
    4. Improving accuracy of perceptions of member interactions.
    5. Improving problem-solving and decision-making skills.

Procedure

A. The group itself will become the object of our study. The initial task will be to develop a learning group through shared decision-making about our goals and methods.
    Utilizing such methodology and resources as readings, projects, tapes, films, role-plays, discussions, videotape recording, and group skill exercises.
B. See attached Bibliography of Books, Phamphlets, and Tapes.

Interpersonal Communication (weeks 7-11)

Purpose: To increase personal effectiveness and competence through the intellectual and emotional understanding of interpersonal, individual, and group behavior, we will focus on the personal growth of the student in self-awareness, confidence in self-expression, greater perceptivity and sensitivity to the feelings and expression of others. *Procedure*: The group interaction provides the learning data which inform each individual about his impact on others. The group affords the experimental setting where new behaviors and relationships can be attempted.

Readings, discussion, and group exercises provide the milieu for these basic learning encounters, which are termed *T-groups* or *sensitivity training groups*.

A weekend at the Outdoor Education Center may be arranged for a more intensive training session.

Logs — a notebook of comments and reactions to any aspect of the course should be submitted weekly for comment.

BIBLIOGRAPHY OF BOOKS, PHAMPHLETS, AND TAPES
(*On 2-hour reserve)

I. Speech Skills
*Anderson, V. A.: *Training the Speaking Voice.*
*Brown, and Van Riper: *Speech and Man.*
*Green, J. H.: *Speak to Me.*
Gordon and Wong: *A Manual for Speech Improvement.*
Hibbit and Norman: *Guide to Speech Training,* Chapters 1, 4, and 5.
Lewis, and Nichols: *Speaking and Listening.*
*Levy, L., *et al.*: *Voice and Speech Handbook.*
*Mayer, Lyle: *Notebook for Voice and Diction.*

Tapes—Audio Visual Collection
Solomon: *Speech as a Creative Medium.*
Basic Systems: *Effective Listening.*
Bell System: *The Science of Sound.*
Goldschmidt: *Ways of Mankind,* "A Word in Your Ear."

II. Group Process Skills
*Bradford, L.: *Group Development,* NTL #1 (pamphlet).
*Bradford, L.: *Forces in Learning,* NTL #3 (pamphlet).
*Lippitt, G. L.: *Leadership in Action,* NTL #2 (pamphlet).
Cartwright and Zander, *Group Dynamics.*
Kemp, C. G.: *Perspectives on the Group Process.*
Knowles, M.: *Introduction to Group Dynamics.*
Miles, M.: *Learning to Work in Groups.*
Student Workbook in Human Relations; University of Kansas.

Tapes—Audio Visual Collection
Conference Leadership (Cantor).
Language: Key to Human Understanding (Hayakawa).
Where Minds Meet.

III. Interpersonal Communication

Bennis, W., *et al.*: *Interpersonal Dynamics.*
Bradford, L., *et al.*: *T-Group Theory and Laboratory Method.*
Callwood, J.: *Love, Hate, Fear, Anger, and the Other Lively Emotions.*
Dollard, J.: *Victory Over Fear.*
Freeman, L.: *Fight Against Fears.*
Fromm, E.: *The Art of Loving.*
Hayakawa, S.: *Language in Thought and Action.*
Hall, E.: *The Silent Language.*
Human Development Institutes, 5 program booklets.
Jersild, A.: *In Search of Self.*
Jersild, A.: *When Teachers Face Themselves.*
Jourard, S.: *The Transparent Self.*
Lindgren, H. C.: *The Art of Human Relations.*
*Maslow, A.: *Toward a Psychology of Being.*
May, R.: *Man's Search for Himself.*
May, R.: *The Meaning of Anxiety.*
Menninger, K.: *Love Against Hate.*
Missildine, W.: *Your Inner Child of the Past.*
National Education Association: *Perceiving, Behaving, Becoming.*
*Rogers, C.: *On Becoming A Person.*
Ruesch and Kees: *Non-Verbal Communication.*
White, Wendell: *Psychology in Living.*

Tapes—Audio Visual Collection
An Anthology of Human Communication.
The Case of Jim
Personal Learnings in Psychotherapy (Rogers).

Appendix B
GROUP PROCESS

Dr. 220T (Weeks 4-6)
T-Th 9:30-12:00 or 3:30-6:00

Assignment: Required readings (to be completed by Thursday of 6th week).

Kemp, C. G.: *Perspectives on the Group Process.*
Sections #23, 25, 32, 33, 34, 37, 40, 46, and 51.
Knowles, M.: *Introduction to Group Dynamics.*
All (77 pages).
Cartwright and Zander: *Group Dynamics,* 2nd ed.
Chapters 1, 3, 9, 19, 25, and 34.

Required observation and report (to be completed by Thursday of 7th
week).
Attend at least two meetings of either the Vietnam Assembly or
Community Council. Type up a short (3-4 page maximum) analysis
of how the group you observed went about its work. You are expected to apply what you have learned in class and what you have
learned from reading in your analysis.

Short paper on group dynamics (due Thursday of 8th week).
Topic questions will be distributed at a later date. Paper should be
5-10 pages long.

Group Observation Forms for Aid in Assignment
on Observation and Analysis of Outside Group

I. You are asked to observe one dimension of group behavior-influence
and control by the members.
Think about how the members seek to control or influence the
activity of the other persons. What did people do as they attempted
to influence others? How did the others react?
Can you identify persons who did not seek to influence the others?
Those who were influenced by others?

Influencing Behavior I Observed   *Reactions in Others*

II. Your are asked to observe several related dimensions of group
behavior—involvement and responsibility of group members.
Do some people appear to be more involved in the group? How
could you tell?
Are some more out or withdrawn?
Do you see some as freer to participate? To what extent was partici-
pation encouraged?
Do some members express distrust?
Are some people forming a relationship with other members?
Do some persons assume responsibility in the group? How did
members take responsibility?

Do some avoid taking responsibility? How? Why?
What actions led you to your conclusions?

III. You are asked to observe one dimension of group behavior—
decision-making procedures.
Decisions in a group may be made with respect to topic selection,
topic shifts, procedures for discussions, etc.
Commonly noted decision-making procedures in groups include the
following:
1. "Plop": suggestion is made but not picked up, resulting in
   decision not to consider proposal.
2. Self-authorized decision: one person initiates action, followed
   by implicit consent and no overt disagreement.
3. Topic jump: drifting or shifting of topic without explicit de-
   liberations.
4. "Handclasp": support of one or two members leads to action.
5. Minority support or vote: majority goes along with unspoken
   reservations.
6. Majority support or vote: one or two more than half give support.
7. Problem census: brainstorming, followed by selection from alternatives.
8. Near consensus: either with reservation, "I'll go along," or with
   the dissent of one or two.
9. Thought and feeling consensus: everyone honestly agrees.
Try to identify the various procedures used in the group at different
points, and their effects on subsequent group action.

Decision-making Procedures I Observed   *Effect on Group*

IV. You are asked to observe one dimension of group behavior—emotions and feelings of the members.
Think about the feelings people are having in the group. What are
some of these? Some persons may not express feelings openly, or
even attempt to cover up their feelings. Look for clues such as bodily
posture, tone of voice, laughter.
Try to identify the feelings you observe in the various members.
How do they express these feelings in their behavior in this group?

Feelings I Observed   *Clues to These Observations*

COMMUNICATION SKILLS & INTERPERSONAL RELATIONS
WHAT TO OBSERVE IN A GROUP*

One way to learn in a lab is to observe and analyze what is happening in one's group. All of us have spent our lives in groups of various sorts— the family, gang, team, work groups, etc., but rarely have we taken time to stop and observe what was going on in the group, or why the members were behaving the way they were. One of our main goals here is to become better observers and better participants.

But what do we look for? What is there to see in a group?

I. *Content vs. Process*

When we observe what the group is talking about, we are focusing on the *content*. When we try to observe how the group is handling its communication (i.e. who talks how much or who talks to whom), we are focusing on group *process*.

II. *Communication*

One of the easiest aspects of group process to observe is the pattern of communication:

1. Who talks? For how long? How often?
2. Who do people look at when they talk?
   a. Single others, possibly potential supporters
   b. Scanning the group
   c. No one
3. Who talks after whom, or who interrupts whom.
4. What style of communication is used (assertions, questions, tone of voice, gestures, etc.)?

The kinds of observations we make give us clues to other important things which may be going on in the group, such as who leads whom or who influences whom.

III. *Decision-making Procedures*

Whether we are aware of it or not, groups are making decisions all the time, some of them consciously and in reference to the major tasks at hand, some of them without much awareness and in reference to group procedures or standards of operation. It is important to observe how decisions are made in a group in order to assess the appropriateness of the decision to the matter being decided on, and in order to assess whether the consequences of given methods are really what the group members bargained for.

Group decisions are notoriously hard to undo. When someone says,

---

*National Training Laboratories Institute for Applied Behavioral Science.

"Well, we decided to do it, didn't we?", any budding opposition is quickly immobilized. We can only undo the decision if we reconstruct it and understand how we made it and test whether this. method was appropriate or not.

A. Some methods by which groups make decisions include:
1. *The Plop*: "I think we should introduce ourselves" . . . silence.
2. *The self-authorized agenda*: "I think we should introduce ourselves; my name is Joe Smith. . . ."
3. *The handclasp*: "I wonder if it would be helpful if we introduced ourselves?" "I think it would. My name is Pete Jones. . . ."
4. "Does anyone object?" or, "We all agree."
5. *Majority-minority voting*.
6. *Polling*: "Let's see where everyone stands, what do you think?"
7. *Consensus testing*: Genuine exploration to test for opposition and to determine whether opposition feels strongly enough not to be willing to implement decision; not necessarily unanimity, but essential agreement by all.

IV. *Task, Maintenance, Self-oriented Behavior*

Behavior in the group can be viewed from the point of view of what its purpose or function seems to be. When a member says something, is he primarily trying to get the group task accomplished (task), or is he trying to improve or patch up some relationships among members (maintenance), or is he primarily meeting some personal need or goal without regard to the group's problems (self-oriented)?

As the group grows and member needs become integrated with group goals, there will be less self-oriented behavior and more task or maintenance behavior. What kinds of categories can we identify?

A. Types of behavior relevant to the group's fulfillment of its task:
1. *Initiating*: Proposing tasks or goals; defining a group problem; suggesting a procedure or ideas for solving problems. . . .
2. *Seeking information or opinions*: Requesting facts; seeking relevant information about group concern. . . . Asking for expressions of feeling; requesting a statement or estimate; soliciting expressions of value; seeking suggestions and ideas. . . .
3. *Giving information or opinion*: Offering facts; providing

relevant information about group concern. . . . Stating a belief about a matter before the group; giving suggestions and ideas.

4. *Clarifying and elaborating*: Interpreting ideas or suggestions; clearing up confusions; defining terms; indicating alternatives and issues before the group. . . .

5. *Summarizing*: Pulling together related ideas; restating suggestions after the group has discussed them; offering a decision or conclusion for the group to accept or reject. . . .

6. *Consensus testing*: Asking to see if group is nearing a decision; sending up trial balloon to test a possible conclusion. . . .

B. Types of behavior relevant to the group's remaining in good working order, having a good climate for task work, and good relationships which permit maximum use of member resources (i.e. *group maintenance*).

1. *Harmonizing*: Attempting to reconcile disagreements; reducing tension; getting people to explore differences. . . .

2. *Gate-keeping*: Helping to keep communication channels open; facilitating the participation of others; suggesting procedures that permit sharing remarks. . . .

3. *Encouraging*: Being friendly, warm, and responsive to others; indicating by facial expression or remark the acceptance of others' contributions. . . .

4. *Compromising*: When own idea or status is involved in a conflict, offering a compromise which yields status; admitting error; modifying in the interest of group cohesion or growth. . . .

5. *Standard-setting and testing*: Testing whether the group is satisfied with its procedures or suggesting procedures, pointing out explicit or implicit norms which have been set to make them available for testing. . . .

Every group needs both kinds of behavior and needs to work out an adequate balance of task and maintenance activities.

V. *Emotional Issues: Causes of Self-oriented Emotional Behavior*

The processes described so far deal with the group's attempts to *work,* to solve problems of task and maintenance, but there are many forces active in groups which disturb work. These represent a kind of emotional underworld or undercurrent in the stream of group life. These underlying emotional issues produce a variety of emotional behaviors which interfere with, or are destructive of, effective group functioning. They cannot be ignored or wished away. They must be recognized, their causes must be understood and, as the group develops, conditions must be created which permit these same emotional energies to be channeled in the direction of group effort.

A. What are these issues or basic causes?
1. The problem of *identity*: Who am I in this group? Where do I fit in? What kind of behavior is acceptable here?
2. The problem of *goals* and *needs*: What do I want from the group? Can the group goals be made consistent with my goals? What have I to offer to the group?
3. The problem of *power, control* and *influence*: Who will control what we do? How much power and influence do I have?
4. The problem of *intimacy*: How close will we get to one another and how personal? How much can we trust one another and how can we achieve a greater level of trust?

B. What kinds of behaviors are produced in response to these problems?
1. *Dependency-counterdependency*: Leaning on or resisting anyone in the group who represents authority, especially the trainer.
2. *Fighting and controlling*: Asserting personal dominance, attempting to get own way regardless of others.
3. *Withdrawing*: Trying to remove the sources of uncomfortable feelings by psychologically leaving the group.
4. *Pairing up*: Seeking out one or two supporters and forming a kind of emotional subgroup in which the members protect and support one another.

These are not the only kinds of things which can be observed in a group. What it is important to observe will vary with what the group is doing, the needs of the observer and his purposes, and many other factors. The main point, however, is that improving our skills in observing what is going on in the group will provide us with important data for understanding groups and increasing our effectiveness within them.

WRITING AND RESEARCH ASSIGNMENT

Choose one of the following topics for a 5-10 page scholarly research report.

Topic 1. *The Effective Group*

What factors influence effective group functioning? How

would you define an effective group? In what situations are different sizes of groups most effective? How is group climate or atmosphere related to group efficiency?

Topic 2. *Leadership*

What is the function of leadership—of a leader? How does a leader relate to a group? Why do some leaders stimulate members; others not? What should be the distribution of authority between the leader and the group members? What is group-centered leadership? What is "effective" leadership?

Topic 3. *Individual Membership*

What group behaviors modify or affect individual behaviors and how? What about the reverse of this? What about self-concept in a group vs. self-concept outside the group; or in one group vs. in another group? How do the personalities of the members and leader affect the character of the group? What are legitimate member roles and functions?

Topic 4. *Group Skills*

What are the practical means to initiate action, to define group goals, to straighten out bogged-down group activity? How are group resources mobilized toward the achievement of goals? What to do about monopolizers, silent members, keeping focus on the point; how to improve communication, minimize tensions, reduce arguments, and assist in the functions of the group.

Topic 5. *Task Groups*

What are task groups? How are problems solved and decisions made so that all members have contributed and the members committed to the decision? How can an unpopular view be presented without disruption? Measure the relative effectiveness of "brainstorming," noting participative decision-making and the "efficiency" of authoritarianism.

Topic 6. *The T-group*

What are the objectives of the T-group? What are the roles of the trainer and of the members? What is the necessary climate to achieve its goals and how is it achieved? What are the purposes of trainer interventions? What are the limitations of the T-group in terms of its objectives and methods? How does the T-group differ from therapy groups? What about time, place, and makeup of the members?

Topic 7. Your choice of subject matter resulting from your readings and after consultation with the instructor.

Appendix C

Q-SORT AND SELF-DESCRIPTIVE QUESTIONNAIRE

Q-sort

1. I like to be the center of attention.
2. People can pretty easily change my viewpoint even though my mind was already made up.
3. I feel that I would be a much better person if I could gain more understanding of myself.
4. I like to help when people need someone to talk to.
5. I have no difficulty in talking to a group of children.
6. I prefer activities where I am on my own.
7. The size of the group doesn't affect my participation.
8. I can't talk freely with adults.
9. I can talk freely with others my own age.
10. It seems to me that I have more problems than others do.
11. My ideal self is far above the "real" me.
12. If you show weakness you're liable to get clobbered.
13. I become impatient with self-appointed leaders.
14. I am sometimes startled to discover that people I admire are "human" and have similar feelings to mine.
15. I usually step in and smooth over a brewing conflict.
16. It makes me uncomfortable to give a prepared speech.
17. I'm hurt easily by criticism.
18. I often get the feeling I'm not really part of a group.
19. I feel timid in the presence of people I regard as my superiors.
20. I dread going into a room by myself where other people have already gathered and are talking.
21. It hurts me to criticize somebody else openly.
22. I like to accept the leadership of people I admire.
23. I find it difficult to disagree openly with majority opinion.
24. I become uncomfortable when conversations get too personal.
25. My voice is expressive.
26. I tend to be on my guard with people who are somewhat more friendly than I had expected.
27. It is annoying to listen to someone who rambles or who cannot seem to make up his mind.
28. I can be open and frank with others.

29. I have a number of close personal friends.
30. In groups I'm pretty much aware of how I come across to others.
31. A good leader shares the leadership.
32. I sincerely doubt if a three-month course can change one's behavior.
33. I can tell a lot about what a person really means by nonverbal cues.
34. I get very nervous when people are watching me.
35. If things aren't going the way I want them to, I tend to withdraw.
36. When in a group of people I have trouble thinking of things to talk about.
37. I'd rather listen than talk.
38. I usually don't like to talk much unless I am with people I know very well.
39. I'm often called upon to settle arguments and disputes between others.
40. I tend to stutter or become inarticulate when speaking before groups.
41. Discussions go so fast I often miss the chance to put in my two cents' worth.
42. Anticipation of humiliation prevents my participation in group situations.
43. I don't get angry at the time but often when it's too late to say anything.
44. I get discouraged if others don't respond to my ideas and suggestions.
45. I don't talk in groups even when I have ideas to express.
46. I don't often express strong approval or disapproval.
47. If a group is silent, I feel I have to do something about it.
48. I am apt to hide my feelings to the point that people may hurt me without their knowing about it.
49. I prefer a structured situation with clear goals and assigned tasks.
50. I can easily put myself in someone else's place and imagine how I would feel in the same situation.
51. I try to understand why different people react in different ways to a situation.
52. I don't see how a group of strangers can function so as to satisfy individual needs.
53. I can express my ideas well and understandably.
54. I always say what I think.
55. I think my ideas are worthwhile.

56. I am not concerned about how others feel about me.
57. It's easier for me to give help than to ask for help.
58. I would never feel right if I thought I wasn't doing my share of the discussion in any group I belonged to.
59. I often say things on the spur of the moment without stopping to think.
60. It's important to participate in group discussion to get anything out of it.
61. I am satisfied with my behavior in groups.
62. I feel I am a reasonably sensitive and perceptive person.
63. I can lead discussions well.
64. My speaking voice is distinct and easily understood.
65. My feelings toward myself will influence my feelings about others.
66. I think that, to communicate effectively, little more is required than willingness and interest.
67. I'm aware of group processes as distinct from group tasks.
68. I feel everyone has similar and not very unique problems.
69. I tend to judge speakers by externals (accents, clothing, mannerisms) rather than by what they are saying.
70. I like to be one of the leaders in the organizations and groups to which I belong.
71. Instead of listening, I often find myself thinking up my next idea or argument.
72. I listen attentively to speakers.
73. I participate easily in new groups.

Self-descriptive Questionnaire

Pre- and Post-Test
Form

Name:

Date:

Communication and Interpersonal
Relationship Workshop. Based on
W. Burke, NTL-IABS.

This form is to help you think about various aspects of your relationships with others and your communication skills in group situations. Read through the list and check the appropriate column that identifies most closely the level of your skill and behavior.

	Low Level	Average Level	High Level
Communication			
1. Speaking in a group	_____	_____	_____
2. Listening attentively	_____	_____	_____
3. Being vocally expressive and clear	_____	_____	_____
4. Thinking before I talk	_____	_____	_____
5. Speaking without fear	_____	_____	_____
Group Observation			
1. Noting tension in a group	_____	_____	_____
2. Noting who talks to whom	_____	_____	_____
3. Noting who is being left out	_____	_____	_____
4. Noting reactions to my comments	_____	_____	_____
5. Noting nonverbal cues	_____	_____	_____
Task Skills			
1. Asking for ideas, opinions	_____	_____	_____
2. Giving ideas, opinions	_____	_____	_____
3. Evaluating ideas critically	_____	_____	_____
4. Summarizing discussion	_____	_____	_____
5. Being able to lead discussions	_____	_____	_____
6. Resolving conflict in a group	_____	_____	_____
Responsiveness			
1. Willing to tell others what I feel	_____	_____	_____
2. Disagreeing openly	_____	_____	_____
3. Expressing warm feelings	_____	_____	_____
4. Sensing others' feelings	_____	_____	_____
5. Being able to accept closeness, affection	_____	_____	_____
6. Being able to tolerate silence	_____	_____	_____
Relation to group			
1. Being accepting of opposing views	_____	_____	_____
2. Acting dominant toward others	_____	_____	_____
3. Being supportive of others	_____	_____	_____
4. Being able to stand up for myself	_____	_____	_____
5. Making snap judgments	_____	_____	_____
6. Feeling part of the group	_____	_____	_____
7. Accepting help willingly	_____	_____	_____
Self-awareness			
1. Understanding why I do what I do	_____	_____	_____
2. Encouraging comments on my own behavior	_____	_____	_____
3. Observing commonalities between myself and others	_____	_____	_____
4. Criticizing myself	_____	_____	_____
5. Willing to find out new things about myself	_____	_____	_____
6. Feeling self-confident	_____	_____	_____